Runes

Divination and Magic With the Elder Futhark Runes

(Unlock the Ancient Power of the Elder Futhark Through Runic Magic)

Trenton Harris

Published By **Kate Sanders**

Trenton Harris

Runes: Divination and Magic With the Elder Futhark Runes (Unlock the Ancient Power of the Elder Futhark Through Runic Magic)

ISBN 978-1-9992826-2-2

No part of this guidebook shall be reproduced in any form without permission in writing from the publisher except in the case of brief quotations embodied in critical articles or reviews.

Legal & Disclaimer

The information contained in this book is not designed to replace or take the place of any form of medicine or professional medical advice. The information in this book has been provided for educational & entertainment purposes only.

The information contained in this book has been compiled from sources deemed reliable, and it is accurate to the best of the Author's knowledge; however, the Author cannot guarantee its accuracy and validity and cannot be held liable for any errors or omissions. Changes are periodically made to this book. You must consult your doctor or get professional medical advice before using any of the suggested remedies, techniques, or information in this book.

Upon using the information contained in this book, you agree to hold harmless the Author from and against any damages, costs, and expenses, including any legal fees potentially resulting from the application of any of the information provided by this guide. This disclaimer applies to any damages or injury caused by the use and application, whether directly or indirectly, of any advice or information presented, whether for breach of contract, tort, negligence, personal injury, criminal intent, or under any other cause of action.

You agree to accept all risks of using the information presented inside this book. You need to consult a professional medical practitioner in order to ensure you are both able and healthy enough to participate in this program.

Table Of Contents

Chapter 1: Runic Scripts

With our information of runology as a foundation, it's time to discover the following pillar: runic scripts. Runes had been used for loads abilities, collectively with divination and magic, however their primary use changed into as letters of the alphabet. Ancient runic artifacts, together with rune staffs carved with symbols, offer us with tangible evidence that runes had been used to shape written language. It is feasible to prepare your know-how of runes by way of way of viewing them through the lens of the three primary runic alphabets: Elder Futhark, Younger Futhark, and Anglo-Saxon Futhorc. Understanding the ones alphabets calls for an outline of the runic script, what it is, and the way it abilities indoors its given context.

Different Runic Scripts

From the 1/3 century to the sixteenth or seventeenth century, Germanic people in northern Europe, Britain, Scandinavia, and Iceland used runes as a writing tool. A overdue arrival within the information of writing structures, the ones pictographs are a long way older than the alphabets they had been covered into. This monetary smash will explore the 3 early runic scripts. As such, it's going to hint their spread and evolution and delve into the tribes and cultures that harnessed them. Let us step toward gaining knowledge of runelore as we discover more approximately their past. Connecting with a mythical beyond packed with electricity and intensity, runes can supply information and belief to our lives in recent times.

Early Germanic

The Elder Futhark is an ancient runic alphabet combining elements from Proto-Indo-European and indigenous Northern

European cultures. It changed into in use till the 8th century AD, after which extraordinary versions of Runic alphabets, like Anglo-Saxon Futhorc, emerged. This script modified into inscribed on gadgets beginning from rings to guns, indicating its widespread utilization in Northern Europe at some point of this era.

At the time of Elder Futhark's emergence, the world changed into experiencing a period called Late Antiquity. New generation, which embody iron guns and gadget, changed bronze inside the course of this transitional length, marking a dramatic shift in masses of cultures' practices. This shift set into motion the Migration Period (three hundred–800 AD), wherein Early Germanic tribes invaded and settled in regions formerly desirous about the resource of the Western Roman Empire, an event now affectionately referred to as "Barbarian Invasions." The early Germanic tribes introduced their writing gadget, Elder Futhark, with them as they spread via Europe over 5 centuries.

The Runic Script Heads Abroad

The Migration Period turn out to be a time of massive cultural exchange in Europe, and with it got here the spread of the Elder Futhark script. This historic Germanic alphabet became broadly followed from Germany throughout Scandinavia, western Europe, and at the same time as a ways east as Poland, Ukraine, and Romania. During this era, the Elder Futhark changed right into a supply of stability for brand spanking new settlers throughout many countries, offering a not unusual language to exchange gadgets and precise mind. In addition, it furthermore supplied a useful link to their shared cultural beyond with the useful useful resource of connecting pre-Christian Germanic mythology with close by Pagan practices at some stage in Europe.

Scholars hint the beginnings of the Elder Futhark, a runic alphabet that originated in a fusion of Roman and Gothic subculture, to an uncertain date among 1 BC and 5 AD. This perception is contested with the resource of the usage of a few who consider that it became first advanced as early as 27 BC. The oldest surviving instance of this writing system is an historic runestone in Sweden that dates once more to the 5th century AD. Aside from providing insight into their basis, this script has lengthy been used as a form of communication and divination through many cultures worldwide, collectively with Scandinavia, Britain, and Germany.

Moreover, ancient runes function a relic of the past and include a bargain statistics. One such artifact is the Spearhead of Kovel, located 30km out of doors of Kovel,

Ukraine, inside the early zero.33 century. The runes inscribed on it are believed to be "thither rider" in Danish translation. This victory rune end up now not supposed as a boast but as an presenting to Odin himself. The outstanding spiritual importance of spears at that component had been deeply embedded in Germanic manner of life, specifically a number of the Goths, who treated those weapons with magical reverence. Through those artifacts, we are able to higher recognize the wealthy mythology and ideals held with the beneficial aid of our ancestors.

Likewise, from the mysticism and mythology of Early Germanic people, runes have long held unique which means that and motive. During the 7th to 9th centuries AD, the Elder Futhark underwent a transfiguration, ensuing in excellent runic alphabets. This period marked the Viking Age's begin, characterised by using

European exploration and colonization. Plus, it became indicated the time while runes commenced out for use for political manner, private reflections, and recollections of normal existence.

Anglo-Saxon

During the Viking Age, the Norsemen pillaged, plundered, conquered, and colonized masses of Europe. In addition to their settlements within the British Isles and Ireland, Greenland, and Normandy, they even reached jap Europe. One of the maximum bold Vikings set foot in North America when they landed in Newfoundland, making them the number one Europeans to perform that. The Norse Peoples additionally mounted ambitious kingdoms and earldoms throughout Europe and Britain. As such, it includes York (Jórvík) in northern Northumbria and Dublin (Dyflin) in Ireland. Along with their way of life and traditions, they brought their unique runic writing gadget with them as they unfold for the duration of northern Europe and the British Isles.

The Celts, originating from the Germanic location, made their manner to Britain as early as 500 BC. Yet, there's no surviving proof of them the use of runes or any writing device. This may be attributed to their quick conquest and colonization with the aid of the Romans, who taken into consideration every person outdoor Rome as 'barbarians' instead of keeping their data. During this era, Latin reigned because of the fact the maximum critical writing device of the British Isles. Despite that, its use turn out to be constrained due to a loss of literacy.

However, in the path of the invasion of Britain in the 5th century AD through the Angles, Saxons, and Jutes, the runes are believed to were documented in history books. After triumphing over the Romans, the Anglo-Saxons stayed generally in England. They moreover developed into what is now referred to as the English race, on the equal time as Ireland, Scotland, and Wales retained greater Celtic have an effect on. The regions managed via the Anglo-Saxons contained abundant proof of rune utilization.

Nordic

As the Elder Futhark developed into the Anglo-Saxon Futhorc in Britain, a change took place at the European continent. Coinciding with the Viking Age came the onset of the Younger Futhark. Although those runic scripts derived from the Elder Futhark, they had some vital variations. The primary difference is that on the same time as more runes had been introduced to the Futhorc, 8 had been removed from the Younger Futhark, leaving simplest sixteen characters. This belief of simplification started out out inside the past due seventh century and changed into finalized around the 9th century at the same time as Vikings held sway over lots of Europe. This period created the shapes and patterns we normally accomplice with runes these days and their maximum renowned wielders: The Norsemen or the Vikings.

Younger Futhark and the Viking Age

The Younger Futhark is thought to were in use for the cause that spherical 800 AD, and its arrival changed the records of writing as we realise it. As it spread rapidly for the duration of Scandinavia and Viking Age settlements, these runes were used by kings, warriors, shoppers, and residents. As such, they use runes for severa motives at the same time as documenting, growing a love letter, or invoking the gods. Subsequently, the rune alphabet grow to be flexible sufficient to be used for a few component a person desired.

Compared to its predecessor, the Elder Futhark, a "mystery" script entirely regarded and utilized by the literate elites for religious features. Yet, this Younger Futhark unfold out literacy and writing to all stages of society. Old Norse persisted as especially a spoken language. However, writing extended significantly due to the arrival of those versatile runes that could do pretty much a few problem.

As the Younger Futhark arose, it modified into divided into dialects. These two are the Danish lengthy-branch runes and Swedish or Norwegian brief-twig runes. The former modified into used for inscriptions on stone. Meanwhile, the latter changed into for regular functions. Yet, each are private and legitimate carved into the wood. Over time, the fast-twig runes superior proper into a miles much less tough model of their lengthy-department opposite numbers. In the tenth century AD, those in addition simplified runes took shape in a dialect known as "Hälsinge" or " staveless runes." This dialect originated in Hälsingland, Sweden. Also, it changed into the fruits of a sluggish approach that commenced out out with Elder Futhark giving manner to its more youthful model. These staveless runes are so named due to the truth they typically leave out their stave (vertical line), making it much less complicated to write down longer texts.

However, attempts to adapt the Younger Futhark runes for ordinary use failed, with Latin subsequently turning into the favored writing tool inside the direction of Scandinavia because the region have end up an increasing number of Christianized. By the 12th century, Latin emerge as overwhelmingly used for writing in

Scandinavia, and the runes reverted to their authentic motive as a 'mystery' script.

Medieval

As the Viking Age neared its close to, the discovery of dotted runes, referred to as stung, ushered in the Futhork, or "Medieval Runes." This new set of runes delivered a dot or bar accessory marker to simplify the Younger Futhark's difficulty of one rune representing multiple sound. The numerous accents super amongst 'i', 'e,' and 'j' runes relying on whether or not or no longer a dot, bar, or not a few thing was present.

By the early 13th century, the medieval runic alphabet were in reality original. This alphabet extended the 16 characters within the Younger Futhark, in the end attaining 27. Those who carved runes, known as runemasters, frequently selected to use and alter current runes instead of make new ones. In this manner, a number of the runes featured in the Futhark have been right now derived from the ones in the Elder Futhark. Although there can be diffused versions amongst versions of those ancient symbols, their esoteric meanings stay usually unchanged within the path of each script.

Chapter 2: The Elder Futhark

The historical Elder Futhark alphabet is break up into three high-quality businesses of 8 runes, collectively referred to as ættir or "clans" in Old Norse. These clans have strong linkages to each other and may be used to shape connections among past and gift. Each business enterprise is wealthy in symbolic which means, depicting historical Norse gods, requirements, and beliefs. As such, the 3 ættir of the Elder Futhark includes the subsequent:

Freyr/Freyja's Ætt

Heimdall's Ætt

Týr's Ætt

Per ætt, which translates to 'own family,' is a hard and fast of runes assigned to a specific god from the Norse pantheon. Fascinatingly, the call of each god fits the number one letter of their corresponding set of runes—the Elder Futhark. Learn more approximately this magical language with the useful resource of way of exploring its super ættir and their divine rulers.

Freyr/Freyja's Ætt

The effective twins of Norse mythology, Freyr and Freyja, rule the primary eight runes of the Elder Futhark. Freyr and Freyja, children of Njord, belong to the Vanir pantheon. This elegance of Norse gods is related to awareness, fertility, and the capability to check out the destiny.

Freyr method "Lord" in Old Norse and is the god of fertility. He have grow to be one of the most respected gods amongst each the Norse and Germanic humans. As the god of fertility, Freyr had energy over a few element that grew, it truly is why he changed into so reputable and prayed to via the Norse and Germanic peoples.

Meanwhile, Freyja way "Lady" in Old Norse and is the goddess of affection and splendor, intercourse and struggle, gold and fertility. She is also the goddess of seiðr (seidr), the Old Norse word for a form of magic that would see into the future and characteristic an effect on it.

Freyr and Freyja's set of runes is known as the ætt of the nurturer - a illustration of lifestyles, love, happiness, and pride. Like tarot playing playing cards, runes moreover have corresponding meanings. Yet, their connotations rely on whether or not or not or no longer upright or merkstave (reversed). Merkstave because of this is not the complete opposite of the particular interpretation; think about it as a shadow to its slight. Not all runes carry a merkstave, in spite of the reality that, because some aren't feasible to inform if they're right aspect up or the incorrect manner up. For rune casting, we are capable of explore the 8 runes of Freyr/Freyja's Ætt and speak their moderate and dark meanings. Additionally, most Norse religions view divination as obtaining notion into one's private increase in desire to seeking to expect future occasions. As such, know-how about Norse mythology can assist parse the ones runes better.

Fehu (ᚠ)

The rune fehu is established to the Norse god Freyr and the goddess Freyja. Also, it serves as a reminder that fulfillment can be performed via tough paintings and attempt in location of definitely counting on appropriate fortune. It moreover symbolizes abundance, properly fortune, and the capacity for boom in diverse regions of lifestyles. Furthermore, severa interpretations of fehu comprise strength, foresight, creation, and destruction. In unique terms, it represents the electricity to convert a present situation into a few thing extra. Ultimately, fehu stands for want, wealth, and pleasure that can be attained even as we take the crucial steps in the route of prosperity.

Fehu, whilst reversed in casting, shows a loss because of one's actions or behavior. It can seek recommendation from losing fabric possessions, property, or conceitedness interpreted as greed, discord among relationships, and burnout. In addition, fehu's bad form need to constitute poverty, cowardice, or being superb by way of duties. All this serves as a reminder to take warning in life and our picks, that might have more implications than supposed.

Ūruz (ᚢ)

The rune ūruz is the second one in Freyr/Freyja's Ætt and dates lower returned to the Proto-Germanic language.

This form symbolizes bodily strength and untamed functionality. When performing face-up in a divinatory casting, it signifies amazing strength and hidden energy. Conversely, its merkstave form consists of implications of weak factor, misdirection, obsession, lust, and violence. Depending on in which it appears with distinct runes, ūruz also can signify records, knowledge, sexuality, sexual desire, or maleness. When interpreted through those various lenses, ūruz shows positivity. Yet, unexpected changes are getting into your existence because of self-formation and a want for conscious moves.

Thurisaz (Þ)

The 'th' of the Futhark, Thurisaz, is concept to mean 'giant,' as inside the mythical creature. Norse gods had been frequently embroiled in a conflict with those powerful beings. Ragnarök grow to be sparked via way of fireside giants siding with Loki and Surtr in opposition to Odin and the Æsir at the apocalyptic war. Interestingly, now not all deities shared this hostility; Thor became half of of-massive and Odin's eldest son. Furthermore, giants have often been related to consciousness, power, and hidden expertise, symbols of divine power that could provide an purpose for why gods so fiercely seemed them.

Moreover, the rune Thurisaz is steeped in statistics and speaks to the energy of duality. It is strongly related to magical symbolism, representing the forces of connection and competition inside the universe. These opposing forces may be used for positive functions. However, they're capable of cause battle, defensiveness, or destruction if unchecked. As a instance of strength and sexual power, Thurisaz is notion to symbolize fertility and out of control aspirations. Understanding this hard dating among extremely good and horrible elements can release greater effective elements of their non-public will.

On merkstave which means, its presence in a analyzing may be visible as a caution of the capacity for betrayal, malice, hatred, or lies to go into one's life. As such, it is associated with feelings of vulnerability. Likewise, it is able to be interpreted as a signal that a few thing is amiss in a unmarried's environment or with a courting.

Those searching out further insight might use it to evaluate if there are any terrible affects located in their lives that need to be addressed. Additionally, the rune has been used for hundreds of years by using the usage of those seeking out steerage about their future and viable consequences. Thus, imparting but a few different layer of significance at the same time as it seems in readings.

Ansuz (ᚠ)

Represented with the resource of the use of the letter 'a', Ansuz is the rune signifying notion and connection to at the least one's non secular self. It may be interpreted as a blessing bestowed upon you or an illustration to definitely be given divine recommendation. Commonly notion to refer to Odin himself, this picture of information and knowledge includes omens of right fitness, fact, and harmony. Additionally, this historic picture is idea for its spiritual steering, symbolizing that one need to heed the recommendation bestowed upon them with the useful resource of way of the gods. Ansuz has moreover been connected to revolutionary conversation, indicating that it could benefit those seeking to create or engage with their target marketplace meaningfully. Yet, whilst its interpretation is reversed, it is able to warn of false impression, manipulation, and terrible feelings which includes vanity and conceitedness.

Raidho (R)

The 'r' of the Futhark, Raidho, symbolizes a journey of physical adventure and transformation. It suggests that you are about to embark on a journey essential to personal increase and evolution. This rune encourages decisive motion inside the route of creating the wonderful subsequent circulate. Also, it relates to the rhythms of life and the manner your rhythm can healthy within them. Furthermore, tracing this rune in grounding rituals is idea to help clean away any horrific electricity preventing you from furthering your journey. Ultimately, raidho speaks to the splendor of discovery and changing views that incorporates touring existence's route.

For its merkstave interpretation, raidho indicates a time of disruption and drawing close disaster. This may be interpreted as a caution that a few factor is ready to disturb or halt your development or journey in life or perhaps foreshadow loss of existence itself. In Norse mythology, raidho was related to trips, communique, and travelling remarkable distances. It modified into furthermore seen as being related to loss of life and the afterlife. This connection to future and future makes this rune critical in divination and information lifestyles sports.

Kaunan (‹)

Kaunan, the 'k' rune of the Elder Futhark, is closely associated with restoration. This interpretation of the rune emerged sooner or later of a duration of magical and non secular practices in Scandinavia.The rune turned into believed to offer electricity and braveness to folks who sought its resource in getting better from infection or damage. By looking more deeply into its which means, kaunan may be interpreted as an invite to boldly bypass towards bodily and intellectual health. Much just like the Kenaz (torch), which many pick, this actual ok-rune indicates new possibilities and a rediscovery of inner electricity.

The appearance of Kaunan in studying or interplay can bring about profound shifts in energy and alternatives. As such, it can constitute both effective and awful outcomes. Likewise, it's miles associated with revelation, facts, creativity, clearing vision, and new energy property, allowing you to create the existence you need. On the shadow problem, however, Kaunan indicates faux wish, instability, loss of illusion, loss of creativity, and coming ailment or infection. It also can portend a breakup or feeling uncovered. Considering this picture's aspects can assist interpret your readings and find out capability personal changes in advance.

Gebo (X)

First rune at the runic alphabet symbol after 'futhark,' Gebo, is derived from the 'g' phoneme and is translated to 'present.' This rune indicates an equilibrium among giving and receiving. Yet, it isn't always restricted to material matters. Instead, it consists of emotional and spiritual objects exchanged in relationships and enterprise organisation contracts. Moreover, it stands for a transfer of electricity which may be beneficial or detrimental relying on how it's miles used. Thus, gebo symbolizes the importance of balancing generosity with assertiveness.

In the context of divination, Gebo can denote a proposal or gift-giving, with an expectation of some problem in move back. It might also additionally advise that an character has given an excessive amount of, essential to feelings of loneliness, greed, or obligation. However, whilst lying in competition to specific runes, Gebo modifications its which means to suggest a lack of equilibrium. As such, it is able to be both self-sacrificing oneself excessively or having to make payments thru no fault of your very very own. In those times, it could be considered as a sign of bribery.

Wunjo (ᛈ)

Wunjo is the twenty fourth rune inside the Elder Futhark. It has been used to symbolize both the letters 'w' and 'v,' with its which means that related to delight, love, fertility, religious reward, and community. Likewise, it brings consolation, pleasure, achievement, concord, and prosperity. But it's also essential to maintain in thoughts that too much of a great detail may be lousy. Hence, avoid turning into overly excessive whilst interpreting wunjo.

Aside from that, Wunjo is assumed to originate in Viking life-style, which related it with the god Odin and his notorious rage. Subsequently, its merkstave version of this rune is a sign of depression. Likewise, it's miles associated with defective picks or alienation from others. In intense instances, it can represent out of control anger, an out-of-manage frenzy, or even intoxication or possession. This rune is stated to signify a kingdom of misconception and mindlessness. It can also signify a lack of manage over one's actions and a disconnection from fact.

With Wunjo, we come to the prevent of the ætt of the number one degree, dominated over thru the "Lord" Frey and the "Lady" Freyja. Like the two gods who rule over it, this ætt includes opposites. In truth, three pairs represent each rune in the word Futhark. Fehu and Ūruz, the domesticated and the wild. Then, Thurisaz and Ansuz, the giants and the gods. Meanwhile, Raidho and Kaunan, the journey (experience) and the illness (statistics). Moving at once to the subsequent aett of the Elder Futhark, let us find out greater factors this ancient alphabet has to offer.

Heimdall's Ætt

Heimdall is defined in Norse mythology because of the truth the watchman of Asgard, the sector of the gods and its discern. Odin gave Heimdall the challenge, the leader god he served faithfully, to sound a horn known as Gjallarhorn when Ragnarök starts offevolved. This serves as an alert that Ragnarök is starting and a warning to all beings in Asgard. Along along along with his function as watchman of Asgard, Heimdall additionally guards Bifröst, an enchanted rainbow bridge connecting Midgard (the realm of mortal guys) and Asgard. To counterbalance, Heimdall's feature in guarding heaven's front is Móðguðr (Mordgud). As such, Móðguðr is a maiden etin who stands protect over Gjallarbrú. This is a bridge crossing the river Gjöll which ends up in hell in Norse mythology. Ergo, Móðguðr tasked with guiding those who've currently died during it definitely so that they cannot go back to the land of the residing.

The parent of heaven and the guardian of hell ruling over this ætt symbolizes exchange, increase, and transformation. These runes can assist make smooth your cause and energy to conquer existence's disturbing conditions. Through the ones 8 runes, you may decipher deeper meanings to your surroundings and use them to manual and inform your alternatives. Learning to study and interpret the ones symbols lets in you to discover hidden layers of understanding that provide notion into our lives. Thus, this set of runes is a splendid deal extra than a easy divinatory tool; it's miles a gateway to self-discovery and enlightenment.

Hagalaz (H)

The first rune on this set is Hagalaz (h), this means that that 'hail.' This rune symbolizes nature's detrimental, revolutionary pressure and things out of doors our manipulate. The manner to keep in mind the 3 ættir is as 3 'levels' of a existence's journey. The first ætt offers with the outside and internal affects that create the person. This 2d set, occasionally known as Hell's Ætt, is ready trying out and difficult to help similarly the individual extend and boom. This is captured from the number one rune—Hagalaz—which symbolizes tempering, finding out, or enduring a trial important to heightened internal concord if the storm may be weathered first.

Hagalaz is the second one rune that does not have a merkstave form. As with Gebo, this does not imply that Hagalaz cannot be interpreted in a 'dark' way, however that it's miles every one-of-a-kind rune that lies in opposition (if it falls with the rune skew or sideways in a casting). If it lies in competition, Hagalaz warns of an drawing near herbal catastrophe or disaster of some kind or form. It can also imply losing energy or feeling powerless to manipulate the ache and suffering for your life.

Naudiz (ᚾ)

The 'n' of the Elder Futhark, Naudiz, suggests a time of need and misery. It is an impediment to fulfillment, prompting you to faucet into your inner power and show extra remedy. Naudiz demanding situations you to control your emotions and act with poise at some point of strife. These tendencies define persistence and resolution in lifestyles. This effective symbol implies survival and presents a unique possibility to hone staying electricity in hard moments. With its origins firmly planted in Norse mythology, naudiz stands out as a example of the adventure in the path of triumph.

On the other hand, Naudiz shows confinement and a lack of autonomy. It can are available in diverse paperwork, from arduous hard work to deprivation and deprivation of important subjects. This will also be interpreted as unfulfilled desires, financial instability, and nearly unbearable starvation. In immoderate times, Naudiz merkstave may also even represent loss of life from hunger or poverty. To further offer an motive for this idea, in Icelandic culture, it changed into believed that when a person had surpassed their limits or faced mortifying situations, their spirit may emerge as a wraith referred to as a 'naudhiz.' As such, they may be compelled to live out the the relaxation of their existence in hideous poverty and deprivation.

Isaz (I)

With the meaning of "ice," Isaz (i) is the rune of assignment, frustration, and looking for a way to triumph over them. The imagery of freezing is the terrific way to interpret this rune. As such, Isaz indicates that you are bodily or psychologically in a state of frozen motion, a block. To rectify this, make the effort out to are searching out clarity from within and put together for what is to return as you get 'unstuck.' Isaz is a rune that complements the that means or interpretation of the possibility runes associated with it within the stable. Also, Isaz has no merkstave shape. Yet, if mendacity in competition, it can be interpreted as egocentric conduct or an over-indulgence in sensual pleasures. Likewise, it is able to be a forewarning of a possible betrayal of agree with or treachery or that plots are afoot in opposition to you.

Jēran (ᛃ)

The J-rune, or "Jēran," symbolizes reaping the rewards of your efforts. Likewise, it may be interpreted to intend peace, prosperity, happiness, desire, and success. Sometimes, it's far known as "jera" and represents the non-prevent cycle of life within the universe. As a brilliant omen, it's miles believed that once this rune seems, it honors appropriate fortune and could deliver abundance in all regions of lifestyles. Additionally, Jēran consists of with it the that means of a "correct harvest" or " appropriate three hundred and sixty five days." Hence, it indicates extra assure for the ones spherical them that their destiny may be packed with masses.

Aside from that, Jēran has no merkstave version. Yet, this rune is often seen as a signal of misfortune and might portend delays or plan disruptions. Those with this rune in competition can assume their right fortune to be unceremoniously reversed without caution. It moreover shows that timing is everything whilst making high-quality modifications. Also, it emphasizes the significance of being organized for the surprising.

Eihwaz (ʃ)

Representing 'y', Eihwaz stands for 'yew tree' and is the start of the second one 1/2 of the Elder Futhark. Symbolically, it represents Yggdrasil, the sector tree. As such, it symbolizes power, dependability, trustworthiness, and reliability. In Norse mythology, this rune is associated with enlightenment and protection. Eihwaz is a sign that you are on the right route to reaching your goals and can benefit them with attempt. Then, in its inverted shape (merkstave), Eihwaz can endorse confusion or weakness. Subsequently, it indicates a need to are looking for readability and advantage inner electricity. Ultimately, this rune serves as a reminder of humankind's potential for self-discovery and increase.

Perthro (ᛈ)

Although the right because of this that of Perthro, represented by using the usage of way of the 'p' of the Elder Futhark, is unknown, its importance is known to be plenty cup. Warriors used this historic cube field to forged masses to decide their future earlier than a struggle. Perthro is related to Orlog, an antique Norse term for "future" or the vital mind of the universe. It represents secrecy, hidden records, and information of our destiny. Some interpret it as figuring out one's course, at the identical time as others maintain in thoughts it a sign of uncertainty. In addition, it's far said that casting masses with this rune served as a manner for Northern Europeans to talk with their gods for the duration of times of disaster and upheaval. Yet, in merkstave readings, perthro suggests the feeling of dependancy and loneliness. For example, it may be seen as a signal of a lack of development, deep disappointment, or emotional malaise.

Algiz (ᛉ)

In the historical runic alphabet, Algiz or 'z,' symbolizes protection and stands for the non secular bond amongst mortals and deities. It serves as a protect to maintain off evil forces and assists in connecting to at the least one's higher self. Likewise, it can factor out an awakening or divine opt for in a single's life. Furthermore, it denotes the significance of controlling strength to keep away from capability pitfalls. Conversely, even as its inverted shape seems in a strong, it indicates hidden risks or dropping get proper of entry to to the non secular realm. Thus, it's far a sign of rejection, suggesting some trouble need to be modified soon.

Sowilō (ᛊ)

Heimdall's Ætt's final rune, sowilō, approach 'sun' and shows achievement, accomplishment, and honor. It additionally speaks to wholeness, extremely good transformation, and the electricity to recognize hobbies. Connecting your better self to your innermost thoughts and feelings, this rune stands as a reminder that the sun's energy may be used to clear away lousy affects. As such, it's miles an logo of spiritual cleaning and renewal. Furthermore, sowilō is idea to deliver get right of entry to to more cognizance and intuition, contemplating a deeper know-how of 1's existence.

Sowilō, in merkstave, indicates a lack of reference to our non secular selves. It need to characterize delusions, misguidedness, and moves on account of terrible suggest or recommendation. When interpreted as an omen, it may suggest that one will face failure in achieving their dreams if they may be now not well belief out. Further, this rune moreover indicates a disconnection from nature. As such, it's miles a blockage to our inherent natural focus and connection to the energetic powers inside us.

As we've got visible, the second set of the Elder Futhark, known as Heimdall's Ætt, delves into the "Great Trials of Life." These runes undergo the weighty fact of self-improvement and our connection to future. They speak of a journey that culminates in sowilō, an internal electricity that offers us the capability to pick our route. With this know-how, we can grow to be absolutely authentic, a success individuals, conquering lifestyles's wonderful trials.

Týr's Ætt

Týr, the god of war and sacrifice, justice and order, and patron of warriors, governs the final set of runes within the Elder Futhark. He turn out to be revered for his cosmic judgment and ethical values and endorsed religious fulfillment. Connected to this is the perception that he had a hand in the mythical heroes from legends or myths. In reality, he's remembered as a picture of installed order and atonement. As such, it makes feel why those 8 runes had been positioned below his protection, for they constitute some shape of war, decision, or peacekeeping inner society. Thus concludes our adventure into defining the superb symbols that make up the Elder Futhark.

Tiwaz (↑)

Tiwaz, also referred to as the rune of Tyr, is a image of justice and honor. It stands for a victory finished through taking the right route of motion. Also, it encourages its fans to take time for self-pondered image. Likewise, to research and find out their strengths and weaknesses. The braveness this rune highlights approach making hard selections with the ability for personal sacrifice to win and reach success. With perseverance and strength of mind, its lovers will in the end emerge tremendous.

For the merkstave of Tiwaz, it shows difficulty in improvement and stagnation. Often, it's far characterised through an imbalance among belief and movement. It is likewise a warning signal of blocked creativity, paralyzing self-sacrificing, or over-assessment. Additionally, it may be interpreted due to the fact the diminishing of passion because of a lack of conversation or injustice that results in separation. Understanding this rune can drastically assist personal boom. For example, it well-known blind spots and indicates how one's life may additionally additionally want adjustment to restore concord and balance.

Berkanen (ᛒ)

The second rune in Týr's Ætt is berkanen. Representing the letter 'b,' this rune approach 'birch' and shows fertility, starting, and boom. It is a rune of liberation or regeneration, renewal, and the begin of some aspect new. Plus, it can furthermore imply that new love is set to return into your existence, romantic or in any other case, and that rich instances are in advance. Berkanen merkstave is a sign of troubles, in particular those associated with family or home problems. Likewise, it is a sign of tension or carelessness, abandonment, or dropping control. Finally, berkanen merkstave warns of stagnation, being sterile (infertile), or deception.

Ehwaz (M)

Carrying the this means that that of 'horse,' Ewhaz is the 'e' of the Elder Futhark. Symbolizing motion, development, and development carried out, it inspires collaboration and trusts in relationships. It additionally represents a strong connection to the ones spherical it. Whether for marriage or partnership, loyalty and faithfulness are associated with this rune. Additionally, ehwaz is an indication of specific fortune and freedom, as it could constitute achievement after a journey or a change in direction. This rune, consequently, serves as an confirmation that every one changes are satisfactory ones.

On the merkstave facet, ehwaz shows restlessness or unease that have to be addressed. This rune symbolizes the need for stability and cautious attention on the same time as converting one's life. The so-known as merkstave is visible as a cautionary have a look at. As such, it may portend sadness as a result of unexpectedly made alternatives or betrayals of accept as true with. The key with this rune is to make sure that any modifications are completed slowly, thoughtfully, and in a manner that honors each the past and future.

Mannaz (ᛗ)

One of the few runes wherein you can at once apprehend the English word derived from it's far mannaz. The 'm' phoneme manner 'man' or 'humankind.' It symbolizes the self, your perception and remedy of others, and their perspectives of you. Mannaz is an indication of friendship and hostility, depicting order in society and form inside the divine. As properly as being associated with intelligence and creativity, this rune indicates that useful aid or assistance will quick enter your existence. Additionally, mannaz has historically been used as a talisman to hold achievement to its wearer. Its reference to humanity offers it extra spiritual strength at the same time as used to invoke specific fortune and safety.

As for the merkstave interpretation of mannaz, it implies mortality and human frailties like despair, fable, and blindness. This photo speaks to the darker nature of our thoughts. As such, those mind encompass manipulation, deceit, or foxy with malicious cause. If this rune seems in your casting, it could represent a warning now not to count on any assist or guidance in what you're attempting to find to apprehend.

Laguz (ᛚ)

The letter 'l,' laguz, approach 'lake' or 'water' and suggests recuperation, fertility, and renewal. It captures the waft of water, at the side of with the tides of the sea, and symbolizes the energy of existence and increase in an natural way. Laguz represents the power of creativeness, goals, and terrific mysteries. Likewise, it shows the hidden depths of this global and the quality under it (the underworld). Finally, it could be seen as a signal of fulfillment or of acquiring some thing you have were given been looking for, but with the equal change of a fee paid.

In terms of its merkstave form, laguz indicates drawing close modifications, often of uncertain nature. It can appear as an unwise choice, stagnancy in life, or even a intellectual disorder. Though no longer always terrible, it could recommend an drawing near period of problem. Yet, it may constitute an opportunity to confront fears and take risks that would bring about personal boom and transformation.

Inguz (◊)

Inguz, the 'ŋ' phoneme, is the rune representing the god Ing. This is an older call for Freyr, the god of Earth. Inguz is a sign of fertility for men, of developing internally, or of a time for relaxation and healing. It represents shared virtues or commonplace sense, own family bonds, and the warmth of humankind. If inguz seems in your casting, that could be a sign that you ought to listen for your internal self and are organized to shut off free ends and head in a brand new life route. However, no longer like different runes, inguz has no merkstave form at the identical time as mendacity in competition. Instead, if interpreted, it indicates the idea of try with none obvious trade or tangible reward.

Chapter 3: History of the Younger Futhark

Late in 700 AD, the Viking Age commenced. During this time, there was a mass change inside the worldwide. For example, Scandinavian and Germanic human beings, or the Vikings, conquered masses of Europe and Great Britain. With this age of expansion and exploration moreover got here a change within the language of these raiders, pillagers, and conquerors from Proto-Norse to Old Norse. Also, historic northern cultures shifted from the tough to understand Elder Futhark, used for personal runemasters, to the Younger Futhark, a much greater tremendous and on hand writing device.

As literacy flourished maximum of the Norse humans within the ninth century AD, so did the use of the Younger Futhark. Though there has been some overlap some of the Elder and Younger Futhark symbols from 650 to 800 AD, the Elder Futhark in the end succumbed to its successor. The Younger Futhark modified into higher appropriate for the instances. Also, the Vikings applied it in subjects each extreme and mild. As such, it come to be carried out in exchange files, diplomatic correspondences, poems, jests, and private messages.

Long-Branch Runes

While the Younger Futhark is the decision for the runic script, some variations have been determined. The oldest of these is called the Danish lengthy-department runes. This department-rune originated in and spherical cutting-edge-day Denmark, the ancestral domestic of the Danes. Primarily, they had been carved on stone and are the more complex variations of the Younger Futhark runes. Yet, they'll be nevertheless less hard than those of the Elder Futhark due to the fact they only have one vertical line referred to as a 'stave.'

Short-Twig Runes

Developing after the Danish lengthy-branch runes got here to the short-twig version of the Younger Futhark runic script. Primarily applied in Sweden and Norway, those runes had been much less complicated to carve. Also, in evaluation to their prolonged-branch contrary numbers, they were formed with out a whole vertical stave. During the prevent of the Viking Age, quick-twig runes became greater well-known, continuing in use even into medieval instances. Besides that, they may be taken into consideration the short-hand or cursive version of the runes. Due to that, scribes and shoppers favored them, as they were a whole lot less complicated and faster to carve. Moreover, they may be furthermore called the Rök runes. As such, they are named after the Rök runestone, the longest runic inscription engraved on the stone.

The Runes of the Younger Futhark

Runes had been used to forged spells and were believed to symbolize strength, protection, and real fulfillment. These runes had been inscribed on amulets and jewellery the Viking human beings wore. Furthermore, Norse mythology frequently describes the runes as a language the gods gave to humanity. The Codex Sangallensis 878 is an illustrated manuscript expected to date again to spherical 830 AD. As such, it consists of 24 stanzas associated with the runes of the Younger Futhark.

This codex, recorded in a monastery in Switzerland, includes many alphabets of the historic global. On web page 321 is the Abecedarium Nordmannicum, 3 strains offering the runes of the Younger Futhark. On the same net net page are the runes of the Anglo-Saxon Futhorc. However, this recording does no longer deliver us a proof of the meanings of the runes. For that, we appeared to the Icelandic Rune Poem recorded within the 15th century and translated into English via B. Dickens in 1915.

Let us delve deeper into the runes and the messages they keep. The Icelandic Rune Poem gives tremendous belief into the which means of every rune within the Younger Futhark. Also, it gives an interpretation for us to ponder and orient our castings. Taking the time to ponder their meanings can open new perspectives on life's questions.

Freyr/Freyja's Ætt

As we stated in advance, the ætt dominated over via Freyr and Freyja out of location its very last individuals due to the truth the runic alphabet converted from the Elder to the Younger Futhark. Two runes, ansuz and kaunan changed in shape. Meanwhile, the relaxation remained the same, despite the fact that their pronunciation differed from their opposite numbers. This is due to the fact the spoken language of the Elder Futhark changed into Proto-Norse. In assessment, the language of the Younger Futhark, the Scandinavian Runes, changed into Old Norse, the language of the Vikings.

Fé (ᚠ)

"Source of discord among kinsmen

and hearth of the sea

and route of the serpent."

(Icelandic Rune Poem Verse 1)

Younger Futhark's 'f' and 'v,' fé represents wealth and abundance. During the Viking Age, 'farm animals' and 'wealth' were considered the same, so this signal have grow to be distinctly regarded. Fé remained intact with its actual which means that for the duration of each Elder and Younger Futhark eras. Forging a link between physical and religious nicely-being, it moreover has robust ties to functionality fulfillment or happiness if solid upright. However, if reversed, it could constitute a failure or large loss. Yet, it despite the fact that offers understanding on stopping catastrophe on this context. In addition to this importance, fé is frequently associated with spiritual boom and prosperity, signifying the reaping of the rewards for hard work and backbone.

Úr (ᚢ)

"Lamentation of the clouds

and smash the hay-harvest

and abomination of the shepherd."

(Icelandic Rune Poem Verse 2)

The Younger Futhark rune ᚢ, additionally referred to as úr, holds a spectrum of meanings from 'bathe' to 'iron' or maybe 'rain.' Yet, it contrasts with its elder model, ūruz, this means that that that 'wild ox.' There had been extensively popular interpretations of ᚢ inside the Elder Futhark. One is ūruz (aurochs), and the opportunity is ūrą (water). Old English and the Anglo-Saxon futhorc live real to its úr rune's this means that of 'auroch.' But when considering Old Norse and the Younger Futhark, ᚢ takes on a modern interpretation of úr (denoting 'rain'). If you need to find out this rune's significance in extra detail, allow us to unpack its enigmatic úr form. Likewise, let us discover how it could have an impact to your divination readings.

Upright Úr is frequently visible as a image of new beginnings and capability. When upright, it signs and symptoms and signs fertility and signs that advantages can also come your manner or a few element unexpected need to get up. On the opportunity hand, in its reversed shape, úr conveys erroneous strain or power and serves as a reminder to stay vigilant. Those bearing this rune are advised to take heed of their environment to protect themselves from unexpected danger.

Þhurs (þ)

"Torture of girls

and cliff-dweller

and husband of a giantess."

(Icelandic Rune Poem Verse three)

Thurs (Þhurs) is the Younger Futhark identical of Thurisaz (þ). It incorporates the because of this of 'huge,' representing the principle competition to the gods in Norse mythology. The interpretation of þhurs is just like the Thurisaz of the Elder Futhark. This is the rune of brute energy and indicates conflict and strength. If reversed in its merkstave form, it's far a caution sign of drawing close to chance or malice.

Óss (ᚦ)

"Aged Gautr

and prince of Ásgarðr

and lord of Vallhalla."

(Icelandic Rune Poem Verse four)

Óss (ᚦ) is the Younger Futhark same of the a-rune from the Elder Futhark, ansuz (ᚨ). They may additionally additionally look and sound super, however every are believed to symbolize Odin, or 'God' in Norse mythology. As such, the óss rune is related to conversation, the capability to carry perception, facts, and best advice. In assessment, its merkstave is connected to deceit and manipulation thru miscommunication or misconception.

Reið (ᚱ)

"Joy of the horsemen

and rapid journey

and toil of the steed."

(Icelandic Rune Poem Verse five)

Reið, or ræið in Old Norse, is the Younger Futhark's model of raidō. It consists of the equal runic shape, sound, and because of this as its Elder Futhark version. This is the rune of the journey or the search for enlightenment, and it method 'riding' in both the physical and metaphorical enjoy of movement. On its authentic facet lies private evolution thru enjoy, while on its lousy is a dislocation from the area's rhythm.

Kaun (Ᵽ)

"Disease lethal to children

and painful spot

and residing residence of mortification."

(Icelandic Rune Poem Verse 6)

Replacing kaunan, the 'excellent sufficient' rune of the Elder Futhark, is kaun, the 'okay,' 'g,' and 'ŋ' of the Younger Futhark. Carrying an appropriate because of this of 'ulcer' and representing contamination and sickness or the curing or avoidance thereof, Kaun is the rune of information carried out thru suffering. Though it's miles known for trouble, the rune Kaun also represents outstanding transformation and readability of vision. When reversed in a casting, but, its meanings turn out to be more ominous. As such, it may be a warning of infection, feeling exposed to vulnerability, or lack of gaining knowledge of from suffering.

Heimdall's Ætt

As stated in the previous financial ruin, Heimdall's Ætt problems beginnings and endings, transformation, and chaos. This 2d set of runes infers an entranceway to heaven, the underworld, or even specific realms. Like the number one ætt, runes had been eliminated inside the Younger Futhark. As such, the ones are eihwaz (yew tree) and perthro (lot cup). Then, one rune from this ætt, Algiz (z-rune), became relocated to Týr's Ætt, being modified into its new ʀ-rune shape. Thus, the final 5 runes in addition provide an reason behind the spiritual adventure related to this ætt.

Hagall (ᚼ)

"Cold grain

and a bathtub of sleet

and illness of serpents."

(Icelandic Rune Poem Verse 7)

Hagall, formerly known as hagalaz (H) of the Elder Futhark, is a rune that symbolizes unexpected alternate. It emphasizes the importance of learning from hardships. Likewise, it highlights accepting the assessments and challenges that accompany personal growth. There isn't any lousy interpretation associated with this rune. However, it is able to every now and then be interpreted as an omen of a pending disaster. The lengthy-branch version of Hagall is '✳,' even as its quick-twig version is '↑.' Lastly, its which means stays unchanged, as it interprets to 'hail.'

Nauðr (↑)

"Grief of the bondmaid

and state of oppression

and toilsome paintings."

(Icelandic Rune Poem Verse 8)

Keeping the same runic form as naudiz and the meaning of 'want' or 'constraint,' nauðr is a great deal the same as its Elder Futhark equal. This consists of the manner to interpret it on your castings. It is the rune of necessity and difficulty. In its upright shape, nauðr represents internal energy amidst misery or confusion. On the opposite, its merkstave form indicates want, poverty, or unmet emotional desires. Finally, the lengthy-department shape of nauðr is 'ᚾ,' whilst the quick-twig model is 'ᚿ.'

Íss (I)

"Bark of rivers

and roof of the wave

and destruction of the doomed."

(Icelandic Rune Poem Verse 9)

The unmarried-stave rune of isaz remained unchanged in its evolution into íss. However, it did pick up every other phoneme to symbolize alongside the way, status for each the sounds 'i' and 'e' within the runic script of the Younger Futhark. Meaning 'ice' is the rune of self-discipline and indicates in search of a manner to conquer demanding situations and frustrations. As a single stave, íss has no merkstave shape. Yet, if it lies in opposition, it is able to be a sign of betrayal, self-targeted behavior, or over-indulgence inside the global's pleasures.

Ár (ᛏ)

"Boon to guys

and accurate summer

and thriving vegetation."

(Icelandic Rune Poem Verse 10)

Jēran (ᛃ), the j-rune of the Elder Futhark, has a charming beyond. Once which means 'exact harvest,' it evolved into ár (ᛆ), which stands for 'lots.' Even extra extraordinary is its shift in pronunciation from representing the 'j' sound to 'a,' 'æ,' and 'e.' This transition from Proto-Germanic to Old Norse turned into probable the purpose of this dramatic exchange. Additionally, the rune served several purposes at some stage in historical history. For example, it could mark critical milestones by using symbolizing natural factors.

While the rune form and related sounds might have undergone an evolution, the which means of the rune remained the same. Like jēran before it, ár is the rune of appropriate consequences from ability, know-how, tough paintings, and precise timing. In different phrases, it's far the rune of reaping what you sow. In its upright form, ár represents success, happiness, or prosperity. With no merkstave form, ár is a sign of a possible setback, awful timing, or a reversal of luck or fortune while in opposition. Also, the long-branch shape of ár is 'ᛏ,' whilst the short-twig model is 'ᛧ.'

Sól (ᛋ)

"Shield of the clouds

and shining ray

and destroyer of ice."

(Icelandic Rune Poem Verse eleven)

As the Elder Futhark had sowilō (ᛉ) to represent the 's' sound, so does the Younger Futhark have sól (ᛋ). Both mean 'solar,' but the younger model had an added that means. In comparison, sowilō represents the elemental pressure of the

68

sun's electricity. Then, sól is the personification of the solar in the form of the goddess Sól. Regardless, it does now not change how it's far interpreted for your castings but adds to its which means, because the sun goddess resides on this rune.

Moreover, sól is the rune of success, success, and wholeness. In its upright shape, this rune shows advantageous trade and which you are on track to achieving your existence dreams. Yet, in competition, as it has no merkstave form, sól suggests a disconnection from your motive or a risk of losing sight of your desires. This rune's brief-twig model is ' '.'

With the rune of the sun comes the stop of the second one ætt. Now that Heimdall's 5 runes are protected, it's time to turn to the final set of the Younger Futhark.

Týr's Ætt

Losing the maximum runes out of the 3, Týr's Ætt gained one back because the z-rune transformed and moved from Heimdall's Ætt to the end of the alphabet. From that, Týr's Ætt in the Younger Futhark consists of 5 runes. Ruled over by Týr, the one-handed god of cosmic judgment and ethical values, this ætt offers with the forces of the cosmos. As the very last a part of the runic alphabet's magical adventure, Týr's Ætt symbolizes the understanding gained from the trials of the preceding ætt. Aside from that, it also represents this understanding being positioned to apply past the self to higher the family, the network, or even human society at big.

Chapter 4: Augmentation of the Earth

and adorner of ships."

(Icelandic Rune Poem Verse 14)

With the removal of ehwaz, the e-rune of the Elder Futhark, maðr (ᛘ) is next in Týr's Ætt. Evolving from the Elder Futhark's mannaz (ᛗ), the meaning and the sound represented remained the identical. Then, best the phrase and the runic form change. With the meaning of 'man' or 'human,' maðr is the rune of human lifestyles and intelligence. It now not handiest refers to humankind as a whole however additionally to the primary man from Norse and Germanic advent myths, mannus. Our essential supply for mannus comes from Tacitus, certainly one of Rome's historians who blanketed the parable of mannus. This mannus is a Latinization of 'mannaz' in his book Germania 10, published in ninety eight AD.

According to Tacitus, Mannus was the son of Tuisto, the divine ancestor of the Germanic peoples, who become the son of Earth. The youngsters of Mannus are recorded in ancient songs of the Germanic human beings as the unique ancestors of many early Germanic tribes. It is in the mild of the original families of humanity with that you must view this rune as a symbol of the human own family.

The runic symbol for maðr, ᛉ, is derived from algiz, ᛉ, the z- rune of the Elder Futhark. Algiz connotes 'safety,' signifying a spiritual bond between people and the gods. An upright appearance of maðr for your castings factors to recognition, capability, assist, or help. On the other hand, an inverted rendering of this symbol alludes to mortality or the difficulties faced by way of humankind. Moreover, maðr does no longer have a quick-twig variation.

Lögr (ᛚ)

"Eddying move

and broad Geysir

and the land of the fish."

(Icelandic Rune Poem Verse 15)

The evolution of laguz (ᛚ) from the Elder Futhark finds a similar form in lögr (ᛚ) of the Younger runic alphabet. Both runes carry the which means of 'lake,' 'sea,' or 'water,' with the same runic form and representing the same phoneme (l). Lögr is the rune of existence strength and purification. It symbolizes the washing away of undesirable or now not-needed parts of ourselves as we 'cleanse' the strength of our lives.

When cast in an upright form, it symbolizes that you are on the right route to achieving your desires. Akin to nature's equilibrium, this calls for a price, a rate to pay for the success you want to benefit. Conversely, if solid in a reversed or 'merkstave' form, it implies difficulties and uncertainty lie beforehand. No brief-twig version of lögr became indicated.

Yr (ᛦ)

"Bent bow

and brittle iron

and giant of the arrow."

(Icelandic Rune Poem Verse sixteen)

With the meaning of 'yew' or, extra specially, 'bow made from a yew tree,' yr (ᛦ) contains the same that means as eihwaz (ᛇ) of the Elder. They are, but, distinctive in their runic shape and the sounds they constitute. Also, it's miles the pastime of the Elder Futhark's z-rune, algiz (ᛉ). Yr captures the exchange in how 'z' become suggested as Proto-Germanic advanced into Old Norse. The z phoneme have become extra of an 'r' sound referred to as a voiced uvular trill, a tough, guttural 'r' sound rolled with the back of the tongue. As such, it's miles written as 'ʀ.' Finally, year (ᛣ) is an inversion of maðr (ᛘ), the existence rune, often referred to as the 'demise rune.' Besides that, this rune marks the only change of letter order the Futhark experienced as it developed out of its elder form.

The Elder Futhark ends with the rune othala (ᛟ), the image of heritage or inheritance. It is a reminder to honor our ancestors through returning what turned into given to us and, in flip, passing it on. On the other hand, the Younger Futhark concludes its runes with Yr (ᛣ), a image representing loss of life and rebirth. ᛣ is etched onto gravestones due to the fact this rune is notion to useful resource souls in their journey past the physical global. In addition, yr additionally indicates embarking on existence's dreams and gaining internal energy. Unlike the alternative runes, there's no 'merkstave' that means related to 12 months, nor does it boast any brief-twig variant.

With the historical rune of yr, representing dying and resurrection, we whole Týr's Ætt and the Younger Futhark. This bankruptcy distinct our know-how of the Elder and Younger Futharks and how to interpret each rune on your readings. Now it is up to you to decide which model you decide upon. The upcoming bankruptcy will discover the captivating Anglo-Saxon Futhorc and one in every of its primary works, the 'Anglo-Saxon Rune Poem.'

Anglo-Saxon Futhorc

The Elder Futhark changed into the unique runic alphabet, representing Germanic languages in Northern Europe. Its evolution into the Younger Futhark around 2 hundred AD marked the start of its use on the Scandinavian and European mainland, where Old Norse reigned best. A sister machine to the Younger Futhark emerged to match a overseas language inside the British Isles. This gadget, known as the futhorc, comprises 33 runes used for Old English.

From the 5th to twelfth centuries, Anglo-Saxon runes have been ubiquitous and served as the main writing machine for Old English. However, with Latin's dominance inside the seventh century AD, runes gave way to their alphabetical counterpart. Nevertheless, futhorc remained famous for divination and protecting spells until the twelfth century.

The futhorc became more developed than its sister system, taking after its discern script by means of extending from 24 to 33 runes. In this bankruptcy, readers will journey thru this final important runic machine. Plus, we can recognize the way it differs from its predecessor and sister alphabets.

History of the Anglo-Saxon Futhorc

In the mid-fifth century, the Anglo-Saxon Migration marked a turning factor in British records. The give up of Roman rule over the British Isles in 410 AD and the emergence of the Anglo-Saxon way of life and those have been good sized occasions in this era. As Rome's grip on Britain faltered, England became among the first regions to suffer its weakening have an effect on. Without Roman protection, neighborhood tribes which includes Britons and Celts rose towards Roman provinces held in England. This brought about a decline in Roman army presence on British soil until their departure.

On the appearance of the Angles, Saxons, and Jutes, they changed Britain's management panorama. As such, they unexpectedly claimed strength with the aid of establishing kingdoms in their own. Before this electricity shift, British Celtic and Latin were broadly spoken, with Latin alphabets used for writing. By the time several centuries had exceeded, Old English changed into hooked up as England's number one language, followed by its awesome writing system known as Anglo-Saxon Futhorc. These tendencies positioned England at a good sized crossroads of records, subculture, and language.

Originating from West Germanic tribes, the Old English language had a lot of influences influencing its improvement. The Angles, Saxons, Jutes, and Frisians all contributed to what later became Old English. A model of the runic alphabet called 'Anglo-Frisian' runes become also heavily encouraged by using the languages spoken inside the regions mentioned.

The Latin alphabet ultimately supplanted Old English and runic script towards the end of the 7th century. As Christianity unfold all through England, Latin soon replaced both because the language of written verbal exchange in the course of this period. Even so, runes endured to be used for divination till the 11th century.

Various texts notice how those changed runic alphabets had been interpreted in a different way across cultures. For example, Anglo-Saxon runes had been used otherwise than their Nordic variants. Some assets indicate they were even employed in anti-witchcraft spells and magical incantations. This in addition highlights how various yet nuanced rune symbols can turn out to be while tailored throughout various contexts and geographical locations.

The Runes of the Futhorc

Like the opposite two runic scripts, futhorc break up into three units of runes referred to as ættir. Each set consists of 8 runes ruled by way of a god or goddess. In addition to getting used for traditional divination functions, these runes can also be used in shielding spells and different magical practices. Furthermore, 9 new runes were introduced to the returned of the futhorc. As such, those offer insights into magical powers and their meanings, which can be explored in addition. Consequently, this phase gives the possibility to delve deeper into all three ættir and observe what the new runes offer.

Freyr/Freyja's Ætt

From ancient times, runes have been used to bring awareness and educate instructions. The first set of runes in the journey of the runic alphabet, Freyr and Freyja's Ætt, consists of opposing forces we come across whilst developing up. It symbolizes the demanding situations a scholar has to bear after they start their esoteric research into runology. This cluster of runes reflects conflicts between domestication and freedom, gods as opposed to demons, and light and darkness. Moreover, the " Gift Rune" and " Glory Rune" at the give up of this ætt aren't juxtapositions however rewards for difficult paintings given to an initiate. A present for the trials faced, and ultimately glory for the prize gained (expertise).

When it involves information how futhorc differs from Elder Futhark or Younger Futhark, there is an Anglo-Saxon rune poem that offers reasons of each rune's that means as our basis. This poem turned into written with the aid of Christian monk Ælfric, also known as " Ælfric the Grammarian," in his manuscript Cotton Otho B.X fol. 165a – 165b around 8th or 9th century.

The knowledge within these runes can be used to train us on how one of a kind symbols constitute extraordinary degrees of boom in existence; it's miles an invaluable useful resource which can manual us through our initiation into existence. With the runes displaying our manner, we are able to use them as gear to master existence's demanding situations on our journey for awareness and glory.

Feoh (ᚠ)

"Wealth is a comfort to all men;

yet have to each man bestow it freely,

if he desires to advantage honor inside the sight of the Lord."

(Old English Rune Poem Verse 1)

From the earliest days of our journey with the futhorc, there's a exact distinction inside the temper that comes through its poem as compared to the ones crafted for the Younger Futhark. While Icelandic and Norwegian rune poems depict fé (ᚠ) as a " cause of strife among guys," its Old English counterpart interprets it as an identical consolation to all so long as they percentage it. This idea of mutual change gives a wonderful evaluation with the concept of sacrifice conveyed by the preceding runic poem.

Feoh (ᚠ) indicates its sister rune inside the Younger Futhark and its ancestor in Elder Futhark at the same time as preserving a comparable form. It is likewise related to 'f' and 'v' sounds, which may be heard from its earliest incarnation as fehu (ᚠ). Representing wealth, this rune symbolizes family aid during our developmental years, reminding us that we sooner or later should pass forth and strive for our prosperity. To clarify this factor, feoh represents our targets despite hardships and adversities.

Ur (ᚢ)

"The aurochs is proud and has amazing horns;

it's miles a very savage beast and fights with its horns;

a exceptional ranger of the moors, it's miles a creature of mettle."

(Old English Rune Poem Verse 2)

The rune úr (ᚢ) of the Younger Futhark has roots in Norse mythology, signifying the strength of self-formation and transformation. It speaks to the capability to apply one's internal energy and change the direction of life, supplying an energizing ability when solid upright. Meanwhile, a merkstave studying denotes domination by using external forces blocking off growth. Connected to 'aurochs,' an extinct wild ox species regarded for its energy and unpredictable nature, this rune gives a effective reminder that with self-determination comes excellent power.

Þorn (Þ)

"The thorn is especially sharp,

an evil issue for any knight to touch,

uncommonly severe on all who sit amongst them."

(Old English Rune Poem Verse three)

A vicinity wherein the futhorc differs from both versions of the futhark is within the which means of the Þ rune of the alphabet. Although it maintains the same sound and form, Þ means 'thorn' in Old English, while it way 'large' in Old Norse and Proto-Germanic. The runes thurisaz (Elder Futhark) and þhurs (Younger Futhark) have been the runes of brute electricity, as well as the connection and opposition between the giants (demons) and the gods. Þorn, but, is a rune of destruction and protection. It represents the sharp "thorns on your facet" that serve as boundaries for you to overcome and grow more potent from.

The historical rune þorn has many interpretations. For example, it could characterize electricity and hardiness won through harrowing reports. Likewise, it foretells a warning of risks and betrayal on the route ahead. However, a few have theorized that its which means 'thorn' is a metaphor for Thor. He is the powerful half-massive son of Odin related to thunder. This interpretation casts þorn as the rune of opposites and brute energy, reinforcing a complicated and amazing symbolism.

Þorn is a image and an instance of understanding from Norse mythology that can be applied to life these days. Its relevance has continued through centuries, offering steerage for seekers who want to understand its symbolic and sensible meanings.

Ōs (ᚠ)

"The mouth is the source of all language,

a pillar of understanding and a consolation to wise men,

a blessing and a pleasure to each knight."

(Old English Rune Poem Verse 4)

The rune of fact and justice, ōs, has two exclusive meanings in the futhorc. The first meaning is 'god,' which refers to Odin in particular. This which means mirrors ansuz (ᚠ) within the Elder Futhark and ós (ᚬ) inside the Younger Futhark. Then, the second interpretation of ōs is as meaning 'mouth.' Such interpretation is every other reference to Odin, who has the "breath of existence," in line with the Poetic Edda. Odin is also the master communicator capable of inspire all and sundry. As such, ōs is the rune of the gods, concept, and communication with others and your better self. Regarding our journey thru the runic alphabet, ōs (motivation and verbal exchange with the gods) is the balance to þorn (barriers and the hazard of demons). Similarly, this is the same as ós turned into to þhurs within the Younger Futhark and as ansuz is to thurisaz within the Elder Futhark.

When cast upright, ōs means that understanding or communique along with your higher self or different powers is incoming. As the rune of inspiration, ōs is a sign that divine energies are interested in you and your lifestyles's adventure. Yet, if cast reversed, ōs is interpreted as a signal of miscommunication, misdirection thru manipulation, or delusion about your dreams or life's reason.

Chapter 5: Old English Rune Poem

While Freyr and Freyja's Ætt ends with kaun, the ok-rune of the word futhark, the futhorc follows the techniques of its discern script and consists of two extra runes in its first ætt. The first is gyfu (X), the evolution of gebo (X), which stands for 'gift.' This is the rune of generosity and stands for same trade, in terms of what you put in is what you get out. As such, it is the 'present' of enhancing your self, improving your capabilities, and experiencing the vicinity to the fullest.

When upright, gyfu suggests which you are approximately to attain a 'gift' of identical period to the sacrifice you have got made to earn it. It also can advise that your vision is ready to clean and that you have the divine blessing to keep. Yet, gyfu does not have a merkstave form. Nevertheless, if lying in competition, it suggests over-dependence or greediness. Also, it is a signal of overly sacrificing oneself for no equal advantage.

Wynn (ᚹ)

"Bliss, he enjoys who is aware about now not struggling, sorrow nor tension,

and has prosperity and happiness and an first rate sufficient house."

(Old English Rune Poem Verse eight)

The rune wynn (ᚹ) is one of the oldest runes within the futhorc, and its evolution from wunjo (ᚹ) is traced to the Elder Futhark alphabet. When have a look at upright, this rune represents preference and concord, symbolizing glory or religious rewards. Alternatively, if sturdy in merkstave, it's far a sign of alienation, lack of records, and capacity risk.

Throughout records, wynn has been related to emotions of contentment stemming from efficaciously the use of one's will or studying a skills. It additionally may be interpreted as promoting accomplishment, prosperity, or fellowship. To further illustrate its importance, it may be useful to say that many Norse tribes could inscribe this rune on their guns earlier than heading into struggle for protection from damage.

Heimdall's Ætt

Once the initiate has handed the checks and alternatives of Freyr or Freyja's Ætt, they acquire the gift of facts and the praise earned for their sacrifices. When they understand this understanding's glory and are to be had to phrases with their reward, the provoke is prepared to transport at once to Heimdall's Ætt, the ætt of turning into a warrior.

Hægl (ᚺ)

"Hail is the whitest of grain;

it's miles whirled from the vault of heaven

and is tossed about by means of way of gusts of wind

after which it melts into water."

(Old English Rune Poem Verse nine)

The rune 'hail' stands for life's unpredictable twists and turns. Think of it like making prepared to move to a modern city and encountering sudden obstacles and opportunities. Turning to the rune form, we see that it's miles a near reproduction of its discern rune, hagalaz (ᚺ), which changed into moreover drawn with a double-barred variant in a few dialects of the Elder Futhark. Moreover, the h-rune of the Younger Futhark, hagall (ᚼ), seems pretty great however includes the same this means that.

Hægl symbolizes the struggles had to end up resilient. As such, it's far the rune of casting, tempering, trying out, and enduring. Likewise, it is like forging a blade that requires ordinary patience and try, and developing robust requires going thru hardships and persevering with. So, with the advent of hægl, the number one rune in Heimdall's Ætt, we're challenged to reveal our electricity.

When hægl seems upright for your cast, it suggests increase and stability. However, it could also be an ominous sign pointing to hazard or loss. For instance, you could be making equipped for a massive circulate, and the rune warns you want to put together for any potential problems.

Nȳd (ᚾ)

"Trouble is oppressive to the coronary coronary heart;

but frequently, it proves a supply of help and salvation

to the youngsters of fellows, to everyone who heeds it betimes."

(Old English Rune Poem Verse 10)

Next, we've got were given have been given nȳd, the futhorcian model of naudiz and sibling to the Younger Futhark's nauðr. The runic shape (ᚾ), which means "want," and sound cost (n) of this rune have remained the equal for the reason that Elder Futhark days. This is the rune of hardships and energy-building. It consists of agreeing with Orlog (your destiny) and making it your very very own. While hægl pushes us with sudden sports, nȳd shapes us into our destined selves.

When forged upright, nȳd indicates an know-how of the essential truths of existence. It is the pressure of innovation and turning into more self-reliant. Conversely, it is able to be a warning of lack or hassle while it appears reversed.

For example, in case you need to benefit your dream profession but hold locating nȳd on your readings, it can mean that you want to assume once more your plan and make a few modifications to get closer to your purpose.

Īs (I)

"Ice can be very cold and immeasurably slippery;

it glistens as smooth as glass and is most want to gem;

it's miles a ground wrought through the frost, straightforward to appearance upon."

(Old English Rune Poem Verse 11)

Another rune that has now not modified loads inside the maximum important runic alphabets is the i-rune of isaz from the Elder Futhark, íss from the Younger Futhark, and īs from the futhorc. All three advocate 'ice' and constitute the rune of energy of mind and popularity. On our runic journey, īs symbolizes the stillness and fortitude of thoughts we have to broaden to maintain our egos in check. After the tempering and molding the closing runes, īs offers with cooling and solidifying. As we advantage more non secular know-how and additional religious reputation through the checks and trials we are going through and triumph over, we come to be greater headstrong. As such, our egos will inevitably grow to healthful our new strengths. Īs serves as a reminder to broaden the strength of will and the stillness of thoughts critical to maintain this strengthening ego in test.

When stable upright, īs is an indication of developing clarity or growing self-recognition. With no merkstave shape, it suggests self-aggrandizement, egoistic behavior, over-indulgence, or other varieties of dropping power of will.

Gēr (◊)

"Summer is a pleasure to guys while God, the holy King of Heaven,

suffers the earth to bring on shining quit result

for rich and bad alike."

(Old English Rune Poem Verse 12)

The Anglo-Saxon picture of jēran (◊), in any other case referred to as the j-rune from the Elder Futhark, is likewise called gēr (◊). This rune has a double which means, with each interpretations being 'right harvest' or 'top year.' Cast upright, gēr represents an acknowledgment for all the tough art work and brilliant moves undertaken. It shows that reaping the rewards of your adventure is simply all through the corner. Additionally, it stands tall as a signal of peace and prosperity.

Unfortunately, being strong in competition can represent terrible timing, stagnation, and regression. Gēr does now not have a merkstave form, which can constitute an lack of ability to improvement due to inconvenient timing possibilities. It consists of elements; a spearhead pointing upwards to encompass success and an arrow pointing downward to signify a lack of momentum.

Ēoh (ʃ)

"The yew is a tree with tough bark,

tough and fast in the earth, supported with the useful resource of manner of its roots,

a parent of flame and a pride upon an belongings."

(Old English Rune Poem Verse thirteen)

The illustration of Yggdrasil inside the runic alphabet, ēoh (ᛇ), is the evolution of eihwaz (ᛇ) from the Elder Futhark. This is a rune that emerge as reduce from the Younger Futhark. Meaning 'yew tree,' ēoh is the rune of life, loss of life, and renewal. It is the rune of the arena tree, the tree of existence. By lifestyles and lack of existence, ēoh does not most effective approach the approaching and leaving from this mortal coil. Yet, it signifies the existence of latest behavior or the surrender of unwanted persona dispositions. In our journey via the runic alphabet, ēoh represents the increase of the man or woman over time. Like a tree sheds its leaves in the wintry weather earlier than growing new ones in the spring, we leave factors of ourselves behind and make bigger new skills as we hold down the route of lifestyles.

If solid upright, ēoh foretells making moves in the path of achieving enlightenment or which you are at the right course to obtaining what you are seeking. But cast merkstave is an indication of dissatisfaction, susceptible factor, or confusion.

Peorð (ᛈ)

"Peorth is a deliver of assignment and enjoyment to the first rate,

wherein warriors sit blithely collectively within the banqueting corridor."

(Old English Rune Poem Verse 14)

The p-rune of the Futhorc is Peorð (ᛈ), which evolved from its precursor, perthro (ᛈ), a rune that does not seem inside the Younger Futhark. As such, its closest cutting-edge English translation is an identical phrase for 'lot cup,' utilized by Vikings to play a endeavor of destiny. This particular rune encompasses the functionality, possibilities, and correct fortune that all and sundry critiques on their life adventure. If peorð seems right thing up, it forecasts real fortune and fulfillment. However, at the same time as reversed, it symptoms hardships past our control.

Eolh (ᛉ)

"The eolh-sedge is usually to be located in a marsh;

it grows within the water and makes a ghastly wound,

overlaying with blood every warrior who touches it."

(Old English Rune Poem Verse 15)

After the peorð rune comes the x-rune of the futhorc, eolh (ᛉ). This picture includes a deeply spiritual and protective this means that. It is the Anglo-Saxon equivalent of the Elder Futhark's z-rune, algiz (Y), on the equal time as its more more youthful counterpart is the ʀ-rune, 12 months (ᛦ). These three runes have one-of-a-type names and meanings: algiz and eolh being 'elk,' at the same time as one year interprets to 'yew.' While this rune can be visible as a sign of loss of existence in the Younger Futhark, it indicates rebirth and protection in Elder and Anglo-Saxon runic scripts.

Chapter 6: Welcoming the All Father

Welcome to a journey via the labyrinthine geographical regions of Norse mythology, spirituality, and divination. As you switch those pages, you can come across Odin, the Allfather, and the runes—mystical symbols that now not pleasant represent an historic alphabet but moreover function keys to know-how the arena spherical and within us. This e-book, "Odin and the Runes: Norse Wisdom and Divination," is your associate guide on an intensive exploration of these charming topics.

Who is Odin?

Odin, often called the Allfather in Norse mythology, stands as a complicated and multifaceted deity. While his titles which include "Allfather" can also recommend a paternalistic figure, Odin isn't confined to that unmarried function. He is the god of know-how, conflict, poetry, and magic, simply to name a number of his manifold domains. His individual is tinged with paradoxes; he's a seeker of information who paid an substantial non-public price for records, and a struggle god who locations the pursuit of intelligence and understanding above brute pressure. He's a celestial discern with very human complexities and contradictions, making him one of the maximum compelling characters in mythological literature.

The Power and Mystery of Runes

Runes, the alternative protagonist of this e-book, aren't mere letters, but vessels of deeper meanings and energies. Originating from the Proto-Norse period, the runic alphabet referred to as the Elder Futhark become implemented for various capabilities, from mundane inscriptions to magical practices. Runes provide a rich problem of have a have a look at on their very personal but emerge as even greater exciting while visible via the lens of their relationship with Odin, who, consistent with lore, determined them in a self-imposed ordeal, hanging from the World Tree, Yggdrasil.

Purpose of This Book

This e-book targets to characteristic a whole manual for all and sundry interested in Odin, runes, and the manner those topics intertwine to offer a notable tapestry of Norse cosmology, spirituality, and understanding. While the hassle remember extensive variety also can from time to time undertaking into complicated territory, the goal is to make it reachable to readers of severa tiers of familiarity with those topics. The chapters are organized in a gradient way, beginning from introductory standards, intending through intermediate-degree discussions, and in the end culminating in advanced theories and practices.

As you delve into subsequent chapters, you will now not handiest advantage historic and cultural insights but furthermore learn how to have interaction with the ones age-antique symbols and traditions in a modern context. Whether you are a non secular seeker, a pupil of mythology, or genuinely someone inquisitive about the Norse way of existence and its mystic symbols, this e-book interests to provide a well-rounded know-how that marries the educational with the experiential.

By the time you obtain the prevent of this ebook, you need to have a robust information of who Odin is, what the runes represent, and the manner you can consist of this historic information into your modern lifestyles. While the purpose is to be as comprehensive as feasible, that is a problem of study complete of limitless avenues for exploration and private engagement.

In the panoramic view of Norse mythology, Odin occupies a regal, crucial position. Known via many epithets, together with Allfather, the High One, and the Raven God, Odin is a complex figure whose have an effect on permeates the cultural, spiritual, and mythological landscapes of the Norse global. This bankruptcy goals to offer a fundamental knowledge of who Odin modified into in the framework of Norse ideals, touching upon his origins, attributes, roles, and own family connections.

Odin's Origins and Characteristics

Odin is predominantly considered a member of the Aesir tribe of gods, even though a few payments moreover hyperlink him to the Vanir. A multi-faceted deity, he is both a god of war and dying, further to poetry and knowledge. Odin became frequently idea to be looking for information and energy, even sacrificing an eye fixed at Mímir's well in change for know-how.

Physically, Odin is frequently depicted as an older man with a protracted, flowing beard, a unmarried piercing eye, and garbed in a cloak and hat. These portrayals aren't just revolutionary conventions however carry symbolic weight. The single eye represents his sacrifice for expertise, whilst his cloak and hat are indicative of his wandering nature, each metaphysical and literal.

Roles in Mythology and Worship

Odin's roles internal Norse mythology are appreciably severa. As Allfather, he's visible as the daddy of many gods, which encompass Thor and Balder, making him the patriarch of the Aesir gods. In the cosmological narrative, he is one of the trio of gods, along together along with his brothers Vili and Vé, chargeable for the arrival of the region and those.

His function extends into the area of mortality via his affiliation with valiant warriors. As a god of struggle, Odin gets fallen heroes in Valhalla, his corridor in Asgard, wherein they put together for Ragnarok, the very last cosmic warfare. On the other hand, his poetic detail is highlighted via his relentless quest for the mead of poetry, a drink that bestows the present of eloquence and expertise. This twin nature makes him a god of contrasts: a god of every creation and destruction, of every lifestyles and the afterlife.

Worship of Odin changed into complicated and variegated. Ritualistic animal and sometimes human sacrifices have been offered to him, especially earlier than big battles, to make sure victory. Skaldic and

Eddic poetry frequently invoked his call, and symbology together with the Valknut (a photo at the side of 3 interlocked triangles) have been associated with him.

Family Connections: The Aesir and Beyond

Odin's familial connections extend his have an effect on and attributes further. He is married to Frigg, and his many children embody no longer truely gods of physical should possibly like Thor, however additionally gods associated with splendor and mild, like Balder. Odin's relationships collectively along with his family people often function narrative devices to discover outstanding virtues and traumatic situations. For example, his deep emotional bond alongside alongside together with his son Balder is examined while Balder is doomed to die, placing Odin on a quest to alter future, albeit unsuccessfully.

Furthermore, Odin's animal companions, ravens named Huginn (perception) and Muninn (reminiscence), and his wolves, Geri and Freki, are symbolic extensions of his attributes of knowledge and war. They roam the sector and the battlefield, respectively, and produce facts to him, therefore serving as his eyes and ears in the worlds.

In the grand tapestry of Norse mythology, the cosmology—comprising of the Nine Worlds—holds a precious characteristic. These realms are not genuinely precis areas, however they function the very skeleton of the mythological universe, putting in place the backdrop for the gods, giants, and people to have interaction. This financial break desires to offer a foundational understanding of the Nine Worlds in Norse cosmology and the way Odin, the Allfather, is interwoven into this complicated cosmic form.

Yggdrasil: The Cosmic Axis

Before diving into the Nine Worlds, one can't neglect Yggdrasil, the cosmic tree that connects all of life. This large, holy ash tree is often conceptualized as an axis mundi, a worldwide axis round which the cosmos is organized. Its roots delve into various geographical regions, and its branches benefit out to the skies, offering a metaphysical shape that connects the whole thing. Odin, in his limitless quest for expertise, is regularly associated with Yggdrasil. He hung himself from a department of Yggdrasil, pierced via his very non-public spear, to gain the expertise of runes, highlighting the tree's crucial characteristic within the pursuit of records and cosmic information.

The Triad of Realms: Asgard, Midgard, and Utgard

The Nine Worlds may be categorized right right into a triad of geographical areas that represent exquisite degrees of cosmological existence—divine, human, and chaotic. The first realm, Asgard, is the dwelling house of the Aesir gods, collectively with Odin, who presides over this divine realm. Midgard, the second realm, is the sector of people. It is hooked up to Asgard through the Bifrost, a rainbow bridge guarded through the god Heimdall. The 1/three realm, Utgard, is the land of the Jotunn or the giants. It represents chaos and herbal forces which may be frequently in opposition to the divine order maintained via the usage of the gods.

Odin's function cuts throughout those geographical regions. As the Allfather and the chief of the Aesir gods, he rules over Asgard. He is deeply involved within the affairs of Midgard, often roaming the human international searching for information or to meddle in mortal affairs. Utgard is in which Odin often ventures to benefit foresight or conflict the forces of chaos, as represented via manner of the Jotunn.

The Lower Realms: Helheim, Svartalfheim, and Niflheim

In addition to the above-mentioned geographical regions, the Norse cosmos additionally includes decrease worlds which can be less described however similarly big. Helheim is the world of the useless, ruled with the useful resource of the being known as Hel, Loki's daughter. It serves due to the fact the very last resting vicinity for people who did now not die a heroic or extremely good loss of lifestyles. Svartalfheim, the arena of the dwarves, is in which the ones grasp craftsmen live, developing magical artifacts even for the gods. Niflheim is often considered a realm of bloodless and darkness, a primordial realm from which icy mists emanated to fulfill the fires of Muspelheim, some other realm, leading to the appearance of the cosmos.

Odin's relationship with those geographical regions is complicated. While he might now not proper now rule over them, his impact is regularly felt. For example, Odin has the strength to grant passage to Valhalla, an possibility afterlife for fallen warriors, thereby imparting an get away from Helheim. He furthermore has connections with the dwarves of Svartalfheim, who crafted his magical ring, Draupnir, and his spear, Gungnir.

The Elemental Realms: Alfheim, Vanaheim, and Muspelheim

Lastly, we've got Alfheim, the realm of the mild elves; Vanaheim, the home of the Vanir gods; and Muspelheim, a realm of fire and heat. While not proper now below Odin's jurisdiction, those realms are important for information the cosmological narrative. Odin's interactions with the Vanir gods, in particular via the Aesir-Vanir war and next truce, illustrate his diplomatic prowess and position in maintaining cosmic balance.

In summary, the Nine Worlds of Norse cosmology provide a multi-layered, interconnected universe wherein severa beings exist and have interaction. Odin, due to the fact the Allfather, has a complex and nuanced characteristic in each of those realms. He isn't always only a king but a wanderer, a seeker of focus, and a cosmic diplomat who negotiates the diverse forces at play. Understanding the cosmological framework permits us appreciate Odin's multi-faceted individual and provides a broader context for the myths, rituals, and beliefs that encompass the worship of Odin and the usage of runes.

Chapter 7: Odin's Cosmic Family

The Aesir: The Family of Odin

The Aesir are the number one circle of relatives of gods in Norse mythology and live in Asgard, one of the Nine Worlds. They are carefully associated with additives of warfare, regulation, and governance. Odin is the patriarch of this circle of relatives, every with the resource of blood relation and by way of the use of marriage. Odin's partner, Frigg, is considered the queen of the Aesir and his kids, which embody Thor, Balder, and Hodr, also are part of this divine circle of relatives.

The Aesir are regularly in opposition to the Jotunn, moreover called the Frost Giants or actually Giants, who live in Jotunheim. This struggle is emblematic of the Norse know-how of cosmic balance, symbolizing the tension amongst chaos and order. Odin's feature due to the truth the leader of the Aesir places him in direct competition to the forces of chaos, emphasizing his role as a god of knowledge, method, and governance.

Odin himself has complex origins. He is the son of Bor and the grandson of Buri, the primary god, who emerged from the ice in Ginnungagap, the primordial void. Odin, alongside alongside collectively along with his brothers Vili and Ve, are credited with developing the sector and the number one human beings, Ask and Embla, from the body of the slain big Ymir. These mythic narratives not extremely good set up Odin's genealogical credentials but moreover reiterate his crucial characteristic in shaping the cosmos.

The Vanir: The Other Divine Family

The Vanir are the second one own family of gods in Norse mythology, living in Vanaheim. Unlike the Aesir, who are in massive part martial and sovereign, the Vanir are associated with fertility, prosperity, and nature. Notable gods some of the Vanir encompass Njord, the ocean god, and his kids, Freyr and Freyja. While now not without delay associated with Odin, the Vanir have a captivating courting with the Aesir, marked thru every warfare and alliance.

The Aesir-Vanir War is a huge mythological event that had a profound effect on the Norse pantheon. This battle resulted in a truce, accompanied through manner of a hostage change to make sure ongoing peace. Njord and his youngsters were sent to live the numerous Aesir, even as the Aesir despatched Mimir and Hoenir to the Vanir. It have become for the duration of this time that Freyja delivered the Aesir to the exercising of seiðr, a form of magic or shamanic workout, which Odin discovered and mastered.

Odin's Position within the Cosmic Family Structure

Odin's complicated relationships internal and throughout these divine families offer a multi-layered attitude on his individual. As the patriarch of the Aesir, he embodies the requirements of manage and martial prowess, however his interplay with the Vanir brings in factors of fertility, magic, and global family contributors. Odin is regularly considered a god of complexities and contradictions, much like the cosmos he allows govern.

His marriage to Frigg indicates no longer handiest a marital alliance but moreover a partnership in governance, as Frigg herself has her private vicinity of have an effect on and understanding. Odin's connection to the Vanir thru the practice of seiðr furthermore indicates a diploma of intellectual and religious openness, adopting and integrating practices from distinct divine households to decorate his non-public know-how and abilities.

Moreover, the alliances and interactions the various Aesir and Vanir illustrate the Norse rate of organization spirit in variety, acknowledging the strengths and domain names of different beings at the identical time as maintaining one's very own identity and integrity. Odin's function in this cosmic circle of relatives shape exemplifies the ones values, making him a effective image for management, records, and inclusivity.

Odin, the Allfather in Norse mythology, is a complicated and multi-faceted deity, embodying records, battle, poetry, and magic. Like many gods of historic mythologies, Odin is regularly represented through numerous symbols and attributes that capture special components of his man or woman and roles within the cosmos. This financial disaster delves into the ones vast symbols to offer a nuanced records of Odin, laying the muse for the exploration of extra hard requirements in later chapters.

The Spear Gungnir

The spear Gungnir is one of the maximum diagnosed symbols related to Odin. Forged by way of using the dwarves, known as the most professional blacksmiths within the Nine Worlds, Gungnir is described as so well-balanced that it could strike any goal, irrespective of the competencies or energy of the wielder. The spear isn't always exceptional a weapon but moreover a example of Odin's authority and capability to hold cosmic order. The spear embodies Odin's dual nature as a god of every recognition and struggle; it's miles the tool with the aid of using which he enforces his will however moreover an extension of his quest for know-how and understanding. The name "Gungnir" translates to "the swaying one," which may be interpreted as a connection with the ever-changing and dynamic nature of life, a topic that Odin is deeply linked with.

The Ravens Huginn and Muninn

Odin is not often estimated with out his ravens, Huginn (concept) and Muninn (memory), who fly anywhere within the global to deliver facts to him. These birds are not in reality partners however characterize Odin's eternal quest for expertise and information. They feature extensions of his cognizance, permitting him to be omnipresent and omniscient to three diploma. Ravens are regularly visible as liminal creatures, able to navigating every earthly and spiritual geographical regions, and their affiliation with Odin emphasizes his shamanic attributes. The significance of concept and memory inside the human cognitive technique highlights Odin's mastery over the intellectual realm, signifying his deep information of the complexities of the thoughts.

The Triple Horns of Odin

A much less typically identified however though big photograph of Odin is the Triple Horn, moreover referred to as Odin's Horns or the Horn Triskelion. This brand includes three interlocking ingesting horns and is frequently interpreted as a photograph of Odin's quest for the poetic mead, a magical brew that gives the triumphing of poetry and cognizance. The quantity three is large in numerous mythologies and is frequently associated with completeness or divinity. In this context, the Triple Horns need to symbolize the three predominant components of Odin: the warrior, the seer, and the wanderer. Alternatively, they may constitute the interwoven nature of the ideas of statistics, electricity, and creativity, all attributes loved and embodied by means of the use of Odin.

The History of the Elder Futhark

The term "Elder Futhark" refers to a specific set of 24 runic symbols or characters. This runic machine has its origins inside the early Germanic cultures and predates the Viking Age, in all likelihood rising throughout the second one to 4th centuries CE. The word "Futhark" is derived from the preliminary phonemes of the primary six runes: Fehu, Uruz, Thurisaz, Ansuz, Raidho, and Kenaz, as an alternative analogous to how we derive the word "alphabet" from the primary letters of the Greek alphabet, Alpha and Beta.

The Elder Futhark has been decided inscribed on a number of media, beginning from stone monuments to timber sticks, and even guns and jewelry. The great use of this script shows that it had every mundane and sacred programs; it end up used for regular conversation and report-preserving similarly to for magical and divinatory features.

Structure and Symbolism

The Elder Futhark is break up into 3 "aetts," or families, every containing eight runes. The 3 aetts are usually named after Norse gods: Freyr's Aett, Hagal's Aett, and Tyr's Aett. Each aett is idea to have its very very personal thematic cognizance:

1. Freyr's Aett: Primarily related to elements which is probably useful to human life, which includes wealth, protection, and fertile land.

2. Hagal's Aett: Concerned with elemental forces, transformation, and cycles of nature.

three. Tyr's Aett: Focused on justice, regulation, and the balance of energy in human relations.

The runes themselves are some distance greater than smooth letters with phonetic values. Each runic image furthermore has symbolic meanings, generally tied to natural phenomena, social constructs, or divine beings. For instance, Fehu, the first rune within the Elder Futhark, is often related to livestock or wealth. Raidho, some extraordinary rune, indicates a adventure or voyage. These symbolic layers add depth to the interpretative technique while the runes are used for divination or particular esoteric programs.

It is critical to maintain in mind that the relationship the various shape of a rune and its associated meanings is not arbitrary. The shapes of the runes frequently resemble the elements or ideas they constitute. Take, as an instance, the rune Isa, which means that "ice." Its honest, vertical line resembles a unmarried icicle, representing stasis and standstill.

The Connection to Odin

As you deepen your have a examine of the runes, you'll come to discover that Odin is often cautiously associated with them. According to Norse myths, Odin decided the runes in some unspecified time inside the future of a self-sacrificial act wherein he hung himself from Yggdrasil, the World Tree, pierced with the useful useful resource of his spear, for nine days and nights. It modified into after this ordeal that the runes located themselves to him, granting him massive information and magical powers. This mythic narrative underscores the importance of the Elder Futhark inside the framework of Odin's records and the broader Norse cosmology.

It's a relationship that we can discover similarly inside the next monetary disaster.

Chapter 8: The Connection between Odin and Runes

Odin's Quest for Wisdom

Odin's insatiable quest for understanding and knowledge is considered one among his defining dispositions. Though he emerge as a god of war, death, and severa distinct geographical regions, know-how remained an elusive treasure that he pursued relentlessly. In Old Norse texts much like the Poetic Edda and the Prose Edda, we discover bills of Odin's many sacrifices for information, along along with his ordeal of setting from the cosmic tree Yggdrasil and his sacrifice of a watch at Mímir's Well.

However, the most compelling tale that links Odin to the runes is the story of his self-sacrifice on Yggdrasil. According to the parable, Odin hung from the tree, pierced through his very own spear, for nine days and nights, fasting and enduring agonizing ache. On the ninth night time time, he glimpsed the runes within the depths under him. With a final, excruciating strive, he seized them and received their expertise. This ordeal became every a bodily and metaphysical journey, wherein Odin transitioned from a nation of mortal lack of records to divine consciousness.

Runes as Cosmic Keys

In the archaic belief system of the Norse, runes had been an extended way extra than a mere alphabet; they were symbols representing critical forces and thoughts in the universe. Each rune become concept to have its private precise electricity and because of this. For instance, "Fehu," the livestock rune, symbolized wealth and prosperity, at the same time as "Thurisaz," the thorn or large rune, represented chaos and detrimental pressure.

By seizing the runes, Odin failed to truely acquire an alphabet however essentially grabbed hold of the levers of the cosmos. This act enabled him to manipulate the crucial forces of the universe, from future to natural phenomena, giving him an unparalleled function within the cosmic hierarchy. Odin's acquisition of runes emerge as more than a non-public quest for records; it became an occasion that had implications for gods and men alike. Through his ordeal, the runes have turn out to be accessible to divine and human realms, serving as equipment for divination, magic, and guidance.

Moreover, Odin's mastery over the runes solidified his function because the god of understanding and poetry. The Allfather didn't keep the understanding of runes to himself however imparted it to humans, especially to folks that are on the lookout for for attention, which includes shamans and skalds (poets). Thus, the runes furnished a medium through which Odin communicated divine facts to humanity. Those who mastered the artwork of rune casting need to glimpse the material of future and the underlying forces of the cosmos, surely as Odin did.

The Interplay of Wyrd and Runes

Runes were no longer actually static symbols; they were intricately related to the concept of "Wyrd," the Norse know-how of destiny or future. In the mythological narrative, the Norns— goddesses of future—have to carve runes into the trunk of Yggdrasil to weave the fate of the cosmos. Odin's mastery of runes, consequently, moreover granted him some have an impact on over Wyrd, allowing him a role in shaping future, in spite of the fact that no longer absolute control over it.

Runes served as a bridge many of the cosmic and the man or woman, the eternal and the ephemeral. They were taken into consideration to be every constant and fluid, rooted within the material of fact but adaptable to the wishes of gods and guys. The dynamic courting among Wyrd and runes emphasizes the complicated interplay of predestination and free will in Norse thought.

Yggdrasil: The Cosmic Tree

Yggdrasil is regularly depicted as a big, evergreen tree whose branches acquire out into the heavens and whose roots delve into severa nation-states, which includes Asgard, Midgard, and the underworld. Its name is derived from Old Norse phrases, "Yggr," due to this "The Terrible," a call frequently ascribed to Odin, and "drasill," because of this "horse." The name can consequently be interpreted to intend "Odin's Horse," drawing a hyperlink among Yggdrasil and the Allfather. This call takes on an delivered layer of which means while considering that Odin as soon as hanged himself from Yggdrasil in a self-sacrificial quest for knowledge and the runes.

At the apex of Yggdrasil is dwelling an eagle, and among its eyes sits a hawk named Vedrfolnir. The eagle and the hawk are believed to represent better states of attention or divine facts. At the opposite stop, gnawing at the roots, are the dragon Nidhogg and different serpents, which also can represent entropy or the forces that aim to result in decay and destruction. The steady interaction among the ones forces of advent and destruction exemplifies the Norse know-how of the cyclical nature of life and dying, renewal and rot.

The Well of Urd: Nexus of Fate and Time

Situated at the lowest of Yggdrasil, the Well of Urd is a primordial pool of cosmic ability. It is regularly considered the Norse same of the Greek Moirai or the Roman Parcae—the Fates who weave the destiny of gods and men. In Norse mythology, the well is guarded via 3 Norns—Urd (Fate), Verdandi (Present), and Skuld (Necessity or Future). These Norns are charged with shaping future via manner of carving runes into Yggdrasil's bark and casting masses into the nicely.

The Well of Urd serves as a repository of collective reminiscence and destiny capability. The Norns draw water from this well to nourish Yggdrasil, thereby ensuring the cosmic tree's fitness and, thru extension, the balance of the Nine Worlds. The water from the properly, laden with the sediment of cosmic sports, splashes lower returned onto Yggdrasil, signifying the interconnectedness of destiny, time, and the unfolding drama of the Nine Worlds.

Odin, Runes, and the Cosmic Nexus

Odin's quest for data led him to Yggdrasil and the Well of Urd. According to the lore, Odin hung himself from Yggdrasil, pierced with the aid of way of his private spear, for nine days and nights in a sacrificial ordeal. It was then that he determined the runes, the call of the game symbols that keep the energy of shaping reality. Odin's association with Yggdrasil and his ordeal to gather the runes underscore the interconnected nature of know-how, destiny, and the cosmic shape.

Runes are not clearly alphabetic symbols; they are keys to information the cosmos and manipulating reality. The act of the Norns carving runes into Yggdrasil's bark to form destiny mirrors Odin's non-public use of runes to adjust fact, a connection that amplifies the relevance of runic take a look at and exercise in comprehending the depths of Norse cosmology and spirituality.

Odin's Ravens and Wolves: Messengers and Companions

In Norse mythology, Odin, the Allfather, is hardly ever depicted on my own. He is normally discovered with the useful useful resource of two ravens, Huginn and Muninn, and two wolves, Geri and Freki. These animal companions are extra than mere pets; they function extensions of Odin's awareness and will, playing vital roles in his quests for information, energy, and cosmic equilibrium. This chapter will delve into the intricate roles, symbolism, and historic interpretations of these animal partners, imparting insights into how they make contributions to the complex individual of Odin.

The Ravens: Huginn and Muninn

Huginn and Muninn, whose names translate to "Thought" and "Memory," respectively, are Odin's ravens that fly all around the world, Midgard, and go back to him with information. These birds are regularly taken into consideration manifestations of Odin's very non-public highbrow schools, embodying his insatiable quest for facts and expertise.

In the Prose Edda, written thru Snorri Sturluson, it's miles stated that Odin fears the lack of Muninn greater than Huginn. This has been the mission of massive scholarly debate. One interpretation is that while concept may be erratic and ever-converting, reminiscence serves because of the truth the sturdy floor upon which statistics builds. Losing one's reminiscence may imply dropping one's self, it definitely is a much graver loss than dropping the capability to generate new mind. Alternatively, Muninn's loss have to represent the existential angst tied to forgetting one's cultural history, know-how, and the collected knowledge of the beyond.

Huginn and Muninn also feature sellers of Odin's have an effect on, acting at crucial moments to preserve messages or guide heroes. In folklore and historical texts, ravens were associated with war, loss of lifestyles, and transformation, aligning carefully with Odin's role as a god of every know-how and war. The importance of those avian partners extends to ritual practices as properly. In blóts (sacrificial offerings), the arrival of ravens end up taken into consideration a effective omen and a signal of Odin's approval or presence.

The Wolves: Geri and Freki

Geri and Freki, translating to "the starving" and "the grasping," are Odin's wolves and serve a particular purpose than the ravens. Whereas Huginn and Muninn traverse the region looking for records, Geri and Freki stay within the course of Odin, typically at his element inside the course of battles and feasts in Valhalla. Wolves, in considerable, hold a complex area in Norse mythology. They can be every big threats, just like the Fenrir wolf, and noble companions, as in the case of Geri and Freki.

The presence of Geri and Freki emphasizes Odin's warrior element and his rulership over the fallen heroes in Valhalla. The wolves additionally underscore the dual nature of lifestyles in Norse cosmology, a existence of simultaneous abundance and struggle. During feasts in Valhalla, Odin gives all his food to Geri and Freki, maintaining himself totally on wine. This act is loaded with symbolism. It may be taken into consideration as Odin's sacrifice of bodily nourishment for non secular sustenance, echoing his relentless pursuit of expertise even at the fee of physical consolation.

Interconnected Symbolism

Both units of animals have protected symbolism that contributes to the depiction of Odin as a multifaceted god. The ravens symbolize the intellectual and religious pursuits, while the wolves characterize the bodily, warrior trouble. Together, they constitute a stability of thoughts and frame, understanding and movement, perception and reminiscence, and existence and loss of life.

In historical Norse paintings and artifacts, depictions of Odin collectively together with his animal companions are not unusual, symbolizing various factors of existence, divine interaction, and the complexity of the human scenario. They furthermore mirror the Norse knowledge of a cosmos that is interconnected, wherein gods, human beings, and animals percent a mutual impact and destiny.

Rituals and Offerings to Odin

The courting among humans and deities in Norse mythology is a complex tapestry, interwoven with elements of admire, devotion, and reciprocal exchange. Odin, the Allfather, stands as a especially top notch decide inner this mythological framework. While preceding chapters have delved into his role in the cosmos, his attributes, and his connections with runes and exclusive beings, this bankruptcy goals to discover the strategies in which Odin may be venerated thru rituals and offerings. The popularity can be on foundational practices designed for those newly embarking in this religious or spiritual direction.

Basic Ritual Framework

When it consists of honoring Odin, or any deity within the Norse pantheon, it is critical to understand the essential framework that paperwork the bedrock of ritualistic practices. Most Norse rituals involve a chain of steps together with purification, invocation, offering, and last. Here's a sizeable define:

1. Purification: This entails cleaning oneself and the ritual space. Often, that is performed with water, herbs, or even a clean meditation to easy the mind.

2. Invocation: This is the act of calling upon the deity you wish to honor. In the case of Odin, poetic invocations frequently resonate, given his feature as a god of poetry and recognition.

3.   Offering: The crux of the ritual, that is the time to provide physical or symbolic gadgets to the deity. For Odin, offerings can range from poetry to mead to symbolic items like runes.

four. Closing: Once the services had been made, it's important to thank the deity and close to the ritual, commonly by using reversing the steps of the invocation.

Types of Offerings

Choosing the proper offerings for Odin is an act that want to be every considerate and personal. However, there are some traditional factors that frequently discover their way into rituals for Odin.

Mead or Ale

One of the maximum traditional services for Odin is mead or ale, beverages that maintain a unique vicinity in Norse tradition. Symbolically, presenting mead might be visible as sharing a sacred drink with the Allfather, invoking fellowship and information.

Food Offerings

Meat, particularly that of beef or pork, is mostly a welcome providing. Given Odin's function as a god of warriors and kings, offerings of hearty, rich meals are considered suitable.

Artistic and Intellectual Offerings

Given Odin's deep connection to information and poetry, offerings of a extra highbrow or imaginitive nature additionally can be very appropriate. This can be an unique poem, a chunk of art work, or perhaps a tune.

Runes and Symbols

Carved runes or distinctive symbols associated with Odin, which consist of his spear Gungnir or his ravens Huginn and

Muninn, can also feature powerful services, mainly while crafted via the individual making the supplying.

Seasonal and Event-based totally definitely Rituals

While you can honor Odin at any time, there are particular seasonal activities and festivals in which such practices may be more potent. The most prominent amongst the ones is Yule, the Norse midwinter festival, which turn out to be a time to honor Odin due to the fact the Yule Father. During this period, the longest night time of the 365 days modified into regularly celebrated with feasting, toasting, and storytelling—all sports sports that may be covered proper right into a ritual for Odin.

Another large time to honor Odin is in the direction of the festival of Walpurgis Night, frequently celebrated at the eve of May

Day. Traditionally related to witches and magic, it's a night time time of heightened religious and magical activity, making it an auspicious time for rituals regarding Odin's extra magical and shamanic elements.

Simple Rune Casting Methods

In this monetary damage, we delve into the introductory techniques of rune casting, a form of divination carefully related to Odin and Norse spirituality. While we can get into greater complicated techniques in later chapters, right here we lay the foundation on your rune-studying adventure with the resource of exploring easy spreads and the symbolism in the back of drawing runes.

Single-Rune Draw

One of the simplest techniques of rune casting includes drawing a unmarried rune from your set. This is known as the Single-Rune Draw, and it's miles often used for brief belief or to advantage a desired assessment of a state of affairs. To execute this, you could typically area all of your runes in a bag or bowl, recognition on a question or goal, and draw a single rune. The interpretation of the drawn rune will offer you with a right away, albeit rather full-size, solution or guidance regarding your question.

Steps for Single-Rune Draw

1.   Focus on your query and clear your thoughts of distractions.

2.   Reach into your bag or bowl of runes.

3.   Pull out a unmarried rune and vicinity it within the the front of you.

4.   Consult your records of rune meanings or a guidebook to interpret the message of the rune.

The Single-Rune Draw is taken into consideration an super vicinity to start for those new to runes. It lets in you switch out to be familiar with the runes and their meanings on the identical time as retaining the technique honest.

Three-Rune Spread

The Three-Rune Spread is some different foundational method typically implemented in rune casting. It includes drawing three runes and putting them in a line from left to proper. The placement of each rune has its significance. The rune at the left normally represents the beyond or the background of the situation in query. The center rune suggests the winning or current situations, while the rune at the right elements in the direction of the future or the final effects.

Steps for Three-Rune Spread

1.   Formulate your question or aim surely in your mind.

2.   Shuffle your rune set in a bag or unfold them face down on a fabric.

3.   Draw three runes one at a time, setting the number one on the left, the second one in the center, and the 0.33 on the right.

4.   Interpret the runes based totally on their characteristic and the way they relate to each distinctive and in your question.

The Three-Rune Spread gives a greater nuanced analyzing than the Single-Rune Draw however remains approachable for novices. It not exceptional allows you to gain insights into the past, present, and future elements of a scenario, however it furthermore permits you understand the interconnectedness of occasions or factors involved.

Five-Rune Cross Spread

While even though maintaining it distinctly easy, the Five-Rune Cross Spread is a slightly more tricky technique that offers intensity with out overwhelming complexity. Here, five runes are drawn and placed in a go pattern. The rune within the center represents the center problem or the present state of affairs. The runes at the hands of the pass represent influences or factors which might be each supportive or difficult.

Steps for Five-Rune Cross Spread

1.   Clearly articulate your question or purpose.

2.   Shuffle your rune set every in a bag or on a material.

three. Draw 5 runes, putting the number one in the middle, then the following runes in the North, South, East, and West positions relative to the center.

four. Interpret every rune based totally on its function and the manner they collectively relate to your query.

This spread permits for a greater complete information of the scenario handy, taking into consideration a couple of impacts and capability consequences.

Rune Casting Surfaces and Context

The floor on which you strong your runes also can have a symbolic impact. Traditional substances embody animal skins and timber forums, however modern practitioners regularly use cloths designed specifically for rune casting. Some human beings even create their non-public casting boards with numerous markings and concentric circles to characteristic greater layers of that means to the studying.

Chapter 9: Understanding Rune Combinations

While person runes provide a wealth of information and perception, it is frequently the relationships among them that provide the deeper, more nuanced understandings of a situation or question. This bankruptcy will guide you via the art work and generation of interpreting rune combinations in easy spreads, that can provide a greater holistic view than considering every rune in isolation. We'll discover the requirements at the back of the dynamics of rune combos, have a look at a few common interpretive frameworks, and examine the varieties of patterns and relationships which can emerge even as runes are forged together.

Principles of Rune Dynamics

Runes characteristic on a hard and rapid of standards that may be likened to a language of symbolic which means. Just as terms in a sentence have an effect on each specific to create a cohesive message, runes artwork synergistically to form an entire narrative. Here are a few fundamental necessities:

Context Matters: Each rune has a very unique which means, however this which means can shift counting on the runes that surround it. For example, the rune for abundance, Fehu, can mean economic gain or spiritual richness, and the runes spherical it will offer clues as to which interpretation holds weight.

Polarity and Duality: Runes frequently have polar contrary meanings, and the presence of a contrasting rune in a selection can each negate, accentuate, or refine the which means that of its counterpart. For example, the warrior rune Tiwaz may additionally seem with the rune of warfare, Hagalaz, indicating a struggle requiring courage.

Elemental Affinities: Some runes percentage elemental establishments like fireside, water, earth, and air. These elemental connections can provide each one of a kind layer of interpretive depth. For instance, runes with a fire affiliation may additionally moreover element in the direction of fast exchange or motivation.

Common Interpretive Frameworks

Understanding the way to interpret rune mixtures is like learning grammar after acquiring vocabulary; it brings form and depth to your readings. Several frameworks can assist in deciphering the interrelationships among runes:

Linear Reading: Similar to studying a sentence, you could interpret runes from left to proper or within the order you've got drawn them. This straightforward approach frequently works well for short questions or clean eventualities.

Focus and Influence: In this model, one rune serves as the focus of the analyzing, on the identical time as the others inform or effect its that means. This can be beneficial for queries about a number one difficulty matter or trouble that has a couple of aspects or complications.

Pairing: Pairing consists of searching at each rune almost about its right now associates. This technique permits elucidate subtler nuances and can be in particular helpful in complex or ambiguous situations.

Patterns and Relationships

Once you have decided on an interpretive framework, search for patterns and relationships most of the runes. These can offer critical clues and layers of which means that that are not right away obvious. Some commonplace styles to endure in thoughts are:

Mirroring: When comparable runes appear in a range, it regularly suggests that the hassle to hand is wonderful or multi-layered.

Sequences: Occasionally, runes will seem in a sequence that looks to tell a story or describe a device. This can be a effective manual for knowledge the dynamics of a situation.

Contradictions: If or more runes in a choice appear to contradict each other, this can advise a complicated or conflicting state of affairs that requires careful consideration and in all likelihood a unique method.

While it is critical to hold in mind that rune interpretation is as a good deal an art work as it's far a technology, know-how those essential requirements of rune dynamics and commonplace frameworks can substantially beautify the intensity and accuracy of your readings. As you workout, you'll begin to increase your intuitive skills and be able to determine the subtler energies and meanings in rune mixtures. So, permit your know-how of these mind manual you but not limit you. Always live open to the myriad possibilities and layers of because of this that the runes can offer.

Odin's Women: Frigg and the Valkyries

The Norse mythological tapestry is replete with formidable figures and complex relationships. One can hardly ever discover the lore of Odin with out touching upon the essential female presences that enriched, balanced, and complicated his life. The maximum outstanding of those are Frigg, his partner and queen, and the Valkyries, the warrior maidens serving him. Understanding the ones figures no longer most effective illuminates the individual and realm of Odin however additionally gives critical insights into the

Norse conceptualization of femininity, strength, and spirituality.

Frigg: The Sovereign Queen

Frigg is often described because the queen of the Aesir and is considered Odin's spouse. The function she performs is a long way from a trifling assisting character in Odin's grand narrative. Frigg is considered a goddess of marriage, childbirth, and motherhood. In the surviving Norse myths, she's portrayed as clever and discreet, with a penchant for foresight. It's endorsed in some sources that Frigg possessed statistics of the destiny however decided on now not to reveal it. This enigmatic great of understanding however withholding is an expression of a kind of power subtly one among a kind from Odin's. While Odin quests for know-how frequently, Frigg embodies a information that is each innate and reserved.

In Norse families, the female became often the "key-keeper," answerable for the management and distribution of assets. Frigg's sovereignty is similar however on a cosmic degree, wielding her authority with tact and insight. One of the maximum well-known myths regarding Frigg is the story of her son Baldr's death. In it, she takes proactive measures to shield her son by means of extracting promises from every object inside the cosmos now not to harm him, despite the reality that she overlooks the seemingly inconsequential mistletoe. This mistake turns tragic whilst Loki suggestions a few distinct god into killing Baldr with a mistletoe projectile. The tale is every a testament to her power and its limits.

The Valkyries: Choosers of the Slain

If Frigg represents the house and regal elements of femininity in Odin's life, the Valkyries constitute the martial and transcendental elements. The Valkyries are warrior maidens serving Odin, accountable for deciding on who lives and dies at the battlefield. They then escort the souls of the selected warriors to Valhalla, Odin's hall, in which these warriors would possibly useful resource Odin in the very last cosmic warfare, Ragnarok.

The Valkyries are often defined as shield-maidens with swan-feathers and are occasionally related to ravens, paralleling Odin's personal raven partners, Huginn and Muninn, symbols of idea and reminiscence. Unlike the Graces of Greek mythology or the Christian angels, Valkyries are far from being benign celestial beings. They are energetic individuals in fight, identifying the destiny of warriors and due to this the outcome of earthly conflicts. While their duties align them carefully with Odin's warlike aspect, they may be now not mere extensions of his will. Various myths show them capable of unbiased idea, emotion, or even defiance of Odin's needs.

Frigg and Valkyries: The Dual Feminine Principle

The contrasting but complementary roles of Frigg and the Valkyries underscore a duality inside the Norse belief of femininity and its interplay with electricity and spirituality. Frigg's home information and Valkyries' martial valor offer a multidimensional view of girl roles in a cosmos wherein impact isn't always strictly monopolized through male entities.

In essence, Frigg and the Valkyries characteristic mirrors and foils to Odin. They exemplify attributes and geographical regions of have an impact on which can be every similar to and great from Odin's, thereby including layers of complexity to his characterization. Just as Odin can't be decreased to an insignificant war-god or expertise deity, Frigg isn't most effective a mother or queen, and the Valkyries are not honestly warrior maidens. Together, they illustrate the shape of female roles and powers, each a prism refracting brilliant aspects of spirituality, governance, and cosmic balance.

In this exploration, we delved into the jobs of Frigg and the Valkyries, the leader woman presences in Odin's mythic lifestyles. We uncovered that they're no longer virtually peripheral characters however entities that hold their geographical regions of energy and importance. They boom and nuance Odin's personal complexities, enriching the tapestry of Norse mythology in techniques that reverberate thru our information of gender, power, and spirituality.

Chapter 10: Norse Festivals and Odin
Yule: The Winter Solstice Festival

Yule is one of the most identified Norse festivals and is typically celebrated in some unspecified time in the destiny of the Winter Solstice, which falls round December 21. It is a opposition of slight, imagined to mark the quit of the prolonged, dark wintry climate nights and the start of brighter days. Odin is a key discern inside the birthday party of Yule; he's frequently diagnosed with Jólnir and Oski, Old Norse names that discuss with Odin's roles in some unspecified time in the future of Yule due to the fact the "Yule discern" and "choice granter," respectively.

During Yule, Odin is said to manual the Wild Hunt, a ghostly procession thru the sky, located thru his depended on ravens, Huginn and Muninn, further to his wolves, Geri and Freki. The hunt changed into each awe-inspiring and fear-inducing, seen as a convey in of misfortune in addition to a spectacle demonstrating Odin's electricity over the spirits. Fires were lit and offerings made to soothe Odin and ensure a fertile and rich new yr.

Ólavsøka: The Festival of St. Olav

Ólavsøka is a Faroese competition that first of all honored the Norwegian King Olaf Haraldsson, who was later canonized as Saint Olaf. While the festival has in massive issue Christianized connotations these days, its roots lie in older, pagan traditions that blanketed the worship of Odin. The opposition is hung on July twenty ninth and marks the dying of King Olaf at the Battle of Stiklestad in 1030.

Though Odin can also additionally appear a peculiar decide to partner with a Christian saint, the syncretic nature of Ólavsøka makes it an interesting case. Odin and Saint Olaf constitute precise, however parallel ideals of manipulate, bravery, and martyrdom, and every figures have been invoked inside the competition's lengthy records. Chants, songs, and poems approximately Odin have been often recited along Christian psalms, highlighting the manner wherein Odin's mythological presence have grow to be woven into even Christianized Norse societies.

Disting: The Assembly of the Thing

Disting is a conventional Scandinavian meeting or "Thing" that takes place in Uppsala, Sweden, commonly round February. While no longer completely an Odinic competition, Disting has robust ties to the Allfather. The "Thing" became each a market and a jail meeting, and Odin, because of the truth the god of understanding and justice, have turn out to be in reality invoked for truthful dealing and righteous judgment.

During Disting, sacrifices have been made to Odin to looking for his expertise and guidance in governance and change. Odin come to be considered the divine lawgiver, and his effect became sought to make sure that justice prevailed. Poems invoking Odin's virtues have been frequently recited, and talismans bearing his symbols have been traded or talented to invoke his blessing.

Runes in Modern Culture

The adventure into the arena of Odin and the runes has taken us via mythological landscapes, complex systems of perception, and numerous practices tied to spirituality and divination. As we transition from the introductory phase of this complete exploration, this bankruptcy pastimes to shed mild on how runes and Odinist requirements take location in contemporary way of lifestyles. The cultural tapestry wherein runes find out their expression in recent times is as severa as it's far fascinating, intersecting with artwork, politics, spirituality, or even virtual media.

Runes in Popular Media and Art

One of the maximum seen strategies runes have penetrated modern-day way of life is thru their inclusion in famous media and artwork office work. Films, television series, and novels regularly draw from the well of Norse mythology to expand characters, symbols, and storylines. A smooth example is J.R.R. Tolkien's "The Lord of the Rings" series, which incorporates runic symbols every as a part of its lore and in its bodily presentation as text. The reimagining of Odin, Thor, Loki, and unique Aesir gods in present day storytelling, specially in comic books and their next cinematic variations, has rekindled interest in Norse way of existence and its mysterious runes. Artists moreover comprise runic alphabets into their works, whether it's miles inside the form of visible art work, sculpture, or layout elements. The aesthetic and symbolic energy of runes provides layers of which means that improve the target market's enjoy.

Runes in Modern Spirituality and Neopagan Movements

In the arena of spirituality, the runes have determined renewed importance among adherents of numerous Neopagan moves. Asatru, a reconstructionist religion searching for to repair the pre-Christian non secular practices of the Norse people, prominently capabilities Odin and the runes in its rituals, texts, and network sports activities. Wiccans and eclectic pagans moreover integrate rune-casting into their repertoire of divinatory strategies, on occasion fusing them with practices from other non secular traditions. Personal boom seminars, mindfulness retreats, and certainly one of a type New Age gatherings also can provide rune-studying lessons alongside tarot playing playing cards and crystal balls, regardless of the truth that their interpretation is often a protracted way removed from the historical or mythological contexts from which the runes originated.

Modern human beings, attracted to the runes for their aesthetic allure or ancient significance, often wear runic jewelry or get tattoos of their favorite symbols. Whether they see those as amazing talismans or definitely as cultural artifacts, the runes are imbued with non-public which means that resonates with their wearers.

Runes and Digital Culture

Remarkably, the age-antique symbols of the runes have additionally entered the digital global. Video video games, specifically those in the fable and RPG (Role-Playing Game) genres, hire runic alphabets for inscriptions, names, and spells. Games together with "Skyrim," part of The Elder Scrolls collection, characteristic runes prominently in their gameplay mechanics and lore. Even cellular packages now offer rune divination gadget, digitizing the historic workout and making it available to a large goal market.

In the region of cryptography and virtual protection, some lovers consist of runes into encryption algorithms or as a shape of symbolic facts instance. While probably more of a novelty than a big exercise, it suggests the long-lasting fascination with those ancient symbols even in our technologically superior society.

Runes additionally take vicinity in online agencies and social media structures wherein humans percentage their interpretations, opinions, and questions about those archaic symbols. Online boards and social media companies dedicated to Asatru, Odinism, and rune divination permit for the pass-pollination of thoughts, blending traditional expertise with cutting-edge views.

Chapter 11: Odin and Shamanic Practices

In this chapter, we pivot to discover an thing of Odin's worship and significance that extends past mythic narratives and formality observances—his function internal shamanistic practices in Norse manner of lifestyles. Shamanism, a religious exercise that includes coming into altered states of recognition to have interaction with the spiritual realm, isn't unique to Norse way of existence. However, Odin's attributes and the techniques of worship associated with him show a shamanistic underpinning clearly worth examining.

The Shamanistic Qualities of Odin

Odin, the Allfather, isn't always best a god of conflict and focus but additionally a deity related with mysticism and altered states of popularity. His quest for recognition led him to dangle himself from Yggdrasil, the World Tree, to find out the runes. This self-sacrifice and the ordeal of putting is eerily paying homage to shamanistic initiations concerning bodily hardships to gain non secular perception.

Odin's role because of the fact the psychopomp, the guide of souls, further solidifies his shamanistic tendencies. In shamanic traditions, the shaman often embarks on spiritual trips to the Underworld to retrieve out of area souls or benefit information. Odin plays a similar function at the same time as he consults the spirit of the volva, a shamanic seeress, within the underworld in the "Völuspá," an Old Norse poem. Furthermore, Odin's ravens, Huginn and Muninn—concept and reminiscence—act as his emissaries for the duration of geographical regions, a function frequently fulfilled with the useful resource of spirit animals in shamanistic practices.

Seiðr and Spá: Odinic Magic and Divination

One of the most direct links amongst Odin and shamanism is the workout of Seiðr, a form of Norse magic or sorcery that involved divination and likely shape-shifting. Though the exercise is more regularly related to the goddess Freyja, Odin grow to be moreover taken into consideration proficient in Seiðr. This magical workout required getting into altered states of awareness, frequently executed thru rituals concerning chanting, drumming, or different kinds of sonic the usage of, to advantage know-how or accumulate unique effects.

Seiðr practitioners should frequently pass into trances to benefit records or perform magical acts. These trance states are regular with shamanic trips to exceptional geographical regions. Spá, some other shape of divination, is taken into consideration a great deal much less "excessive" but is however every other direction by using using which Odinic figures might also additionally want to get proper of access to hidden statistics. These practices underscore Odin's connection to prophetic records and transformative non secular memories, hallmarks of shamanic traditions.

Another thrilling factor to undergo in thoughts is the role of the "immoderate seat" in Seiðr rituals. A seiðkona (a female practitioner of Seiðr) may frequently take a seat on a immoderate seat or platform, a nod to Odin's immoderate seat, Hliðskjálf, from which he should see all geographical regions. This serves as a metaphorical and practical hyperlink between Odinic and shamanistic practices, suggesting a shared non secular imaginative and prescient.

The Berserkers: Shamanic Warriors of Odin

The Berserkers, fierce warriors dedicated to Odin, offer but another attitude on

Odin's connection to shamanism. These warriors had been stated to go into states of ecstatic frenzy ultimately of battle, making them bold fighters. This battle frenzy, or "berserker rage," also can moreover were introduced about through ritualistic way, on the facet of consuming specific herbs or undertaking rites that altered hobby. While the proper practices stay a topic of instructional debate, the ecstatic states that the Berserkers entered bear resemblance to shamanic trance states. This connection places Odin not certainly within the context of a war deity however as a god who permits transcendental states to benefit extraordinary feats.

To summarize, Odin's multifaceted function in Norse mythology extends into the world of shamanic practices. From his personal quests for esoteric records to his institutions with practices like Seiðr and roles similar to the Berserkers, Odin's effect permeates numerous avenues of altered states of popularity and interactions with religious realms. These elements make a contribution to a extra nuanced information of Odin, painting him not simply as a god of information and struggle, but as a complex deity deeply interwoven with shamanistic traditions. This exploration affords a richer, more textured lens thru which to understand the Allfather and, through extension, the spiritual traditions that venerate him.

The Metaphysics of Runes

Rune Energies and Quantum Fields

One of the maximum interesting strategies to discover the metaphysical houses of runes is via the usage of delving into their courting with quantum fields. Quantum subject concept, a basis of contemporary-day physics, indicates that all depend and forces in the universe upward push up from fluctuations in underlying fields. While this mind-set is rooted in medical paradigms, it can provide a theoretical framework for facts how runes feature at a metaphysical degree. Just as particles can be excited states of a quantum place, one might also want to postulate that runes feature specific excitations or resonances inside the vast subject of interest or strength.

When a runic symbol is drawn, carved, or maybe mentally visualized, it is able to theoretically bring about a particular vibration on this problem, influencing possibilities and manifesting particular consequences. This parallels the shamanic perception inside the strength of symbols and sounds to awaken and command elemental forces. In essence, runes would possibly function as greater than mere cultural or linguistic artifacts; they may be keys to unlocking specific varieties of energy inside the cosmos.

Runes and the Human Psyche

Carl Jung, the Swiss psychiatrist who based analytical psychology, delivered the idea of archetypes—familiar, normal symbols or troubles that emerge in the direction of one-of-a-kind cultures and eras. Jung argued that those archetypes are embedded within the collective subconscious, a degree of the human mind that holds the reports and information shared through our species. From this mind-set, runes can be visible as archetypal symbols that faucet into the deep reservoirs of the human psyche.